		DATE DUE	

Promoting an Integrated Approach to Combat Gender-based Violence

A TRAINING MANUAL

Margaret Oguli-Oumo, Imelda M. Molokomme, Monde M. Gwaba,
Valencia K. D. Mogegeh, Lucia Kiwala

 COMMONWEALTH SECRETARIAT

Gender Affairs Department
Commonwealth Secretariat
Marlborough House
Pall Mall,
London SW1Y 5HX
United Kingdom

E-mail: gad@commonwealth.int
http://www.thecommonwealth.org/gender

Published by the Commonwealth Secretariat

Layout design by Wayzgoose
Cover design by Tony Leonard
Printed by Abacus Direct

Copies of this publication can be ordered from:
The Publications Manager, Communication and Public Affairs Division,
Commonwealth Secretariat, Marlborough House, Pall Mall,
London, SW1Y 5HX, UK
Tel. +44 (0) 20 7747 6342
Fax. +44 (0) 20 7839 9081
E-mail: r.jones-parry@commonwealth.int

ISBN: 0-85092-714-5

Price: £8.99

Contents

Preface

Gender-based violence occurs at all times in all societies. It negatively affects the lives of individuals and the development of families, communities and entire nations. The economic and social costs of gender-based violence are huge. Gender-based violence leads to serious physical and psychological harm. Many people, the majority of whom are women and children are denied the right to freedom, liberty and development. Others are deprived of the right to life through death. The distinction between assault, battery, grievous bodily harm and homicides occurring in public places, and torture taking place in families due to domestic violence is blurred. For how long should nation states allow this situation to continue unchecked?

Gender-based violence is now recognised at international level as a violation of human rights. Many governments have ratified international human rights standards, as well as endorsed declarations, and regional and national plans of action which emphasise a world free of violence. This is commendable, but much remains to be done at national and local levels to translate these commitments into reality.

There is a need to recognise that gender-based violence is a social problem, which should be addressed, like any other development issue, by a range of actors. Hence, addressing gender-based violence should become a concern for all, including politicians at the highest level, government departments and institutions, civil society, women's and youth organisations, the private sector and the media. Current efforts to address gender-based violence should be well co-ordinated in order to provide better services to victims, deal with perpetrators appropriately, avoid duplication and promote optimum use of resources.

This manual is a contribution towards adopting a holistic approach to combating gender-based violence. It aims to promote coherence and development of comprehensive programmes for eliminating gender-based violence. Governments should play a leading role in this struggle by adopting relevant policies, providing adequate legal frameworks and supporting the efforts of non-government organisations working in this field. In addition, the manual aims to assist and encourage all relevant organisations, state and non-state agencies, traditional and non-traditional organisations to work together to reduce this scourge. These include women's human rights organisations, civil society, parliamentarians, the private sector and all government ministries.

The Commonwealth Secretariat would like to express its appreciation of the work of the consultants Mrs Margaret Oguli-Oumo, Mrs Imelda M Molokomme and Mrs Monde Mwala Gwaba and staff members, Mrs Valencia Mogegeh and Ms Lucia Kiwala who tirelessly worked on drafting and editing this publication. My sincere thanks to Ms Florence Butegwa who prepared the model framework for an integrated approach to combat violence against women which formed the basis for this publication.

I would also like to express gratitude to the Southern Africa Development Community (SADC) Secretariat and all the governments in East and Southern Africa, particularly Botswana, Kenya, Lesotho, Malawi, Mauritius, Mozambique, Namibia, Swaziland, Uganda, Zambia and Zimbabwe, which provided us with the opportunity to pilot-test the model framework and the draft manual at regional and national workshops. I would like to acknowledge efforts by Ms Margaret Gittens and Ms Musonda Mwila who serviced the various meetings in the development process of this publication. Last, but not least, special thanks to our copy-editor and designer.

Nancy Spence, *Director, Gender and Youth Affairs Division*

Section 1

Background

Gender-based violence (GBV) is widely acknowledged as constituting a fundamental human rights violation, as well as a constraint to development. It continues to be endemic in different forms, in Commonwealth countries and other parts of the world.

GBV cuts across status, class, religion, race and economic barriers. It occurs in the home, the community, the work place and in institutions. It takes various forms which involve physical, emotional, psychological and sexual abuse, including economic deprivation. While GBV affects women, men and children, women and girls are more affected and therefore constitute the majority of the victims. Armed conflict, the feminisation of poverty, the adverse impact of structural adjustment programmes (SAPs), HIV/AIDS and cross-country trafficking in women, worsen the levels of violence against women. Social, cultural, economic and political realities in different regions, low levels of literacy, limited participation by women in decision-making positions and processes, and discriminatory customary practices have made women even more vulnerable.

Violence has been a feature of women's and girls' lives throughout recorded history, ranging from trafficking, to intimate violation by strangers, acquaintances and family members, including husbands and partners. All societies have forms of gender-based violence that are generally condoned and even reinforced by local customs, norms and values.

It is difficult to assess the extent of GBV because of the variations in agreement of what it constitutes. GBV is also under-reported. While official data is valuable, the data is usually not based on widescale research. Formally reported data therefore becomes a poor indicator of the scale of violence. It occurs mostly in private. In the case of family violence, law enforcement officers are often reluctant to intervene in what is normally seen as a private matter.

The exact causes of GBV are not known, but may be rooted in the inequalities and imbalanced power relations between women and men. Discriminatory social structures with a set of complex cultural values, norms and practices which exist in different societies have also contributed to GBV. The legal framework in some countries that should create enabling conditions is inadequate or non-existent. Law enforcement mechanisms are generally weak.

The consequences of GBV adversely affect the individual, the family, the community and society and undermine the country's economic stability.

GBV continues to exist, despite efforts made by governments, Non-Governmental Organisations (NGOs) and Community Based Organisations (CBOs) to address the problem. These bodies have put in place legislative, administrative, judicial and other measures such as medical interventions, welfare approaches, public education and awareness-raising campaigns to address GBV.

Recently, there have been calls for an integrated approach to eliminating GBV. This follows the realisation that in spite of current efforts at international, regional and national levels, this scourge still continues. The problem is perceived from varying perspectives by different agencies within and outside government. There is little or no collaboration between the different strategies or stakeholder organisations and individuals attempting to address the problem. Consequently, policies, where they do exist, as well as strategies and interventions, are sectoral.

Commonwealth Ministers Responsible for Women's Affairs have discussed violence against women at their triennial meetings, held ever since 1985. The persistent nature of the problem, coupled with the lack of significant progress in addressing GBV prompted Ministers at their Fifth Meeting in Trinidad and Tobago in 1996, to urge governments to adopt an integrated approach to combat violence against women. Governments had earlier endorsed this strategic action when they adopted the Beijing Platform for Action in 1995 at the end of the UN Fourth World Conference on Women.

It is against this background that the Commonwealth Secretariat has developed a model framework for an integrated approach to combat violence against women using Gender Management Systems principles. The *Do It Yourself Manual* is based on the model framework. It has been developed to assist relevant government departments, civil society, community groups and indigenous organisations in their efforts towards the elimination of GBV.

Section 2

About this Manual

The *Do It Yourself Manual* is based on the Commonwealth Secretariat model framework for an integrated approach to combat violence against women. The manual:

- draws on the strengths of the Gender Management Systems (GMS) principles;

- promotes an integrated approach to combat GBV;

- draws on experiences from workshops and consultations facilitated by the Commonwealth Secretariat in Botswana, Kenya, Lesotho, Malawi, Mauritius, Mozambique, Namibia, Swaziland, Uganda, Zambia, and Zimbabwe;

- offers a framework for building on strategies, and concrete suggestions for addressing GBV;

- is a flexible tool that can be adapted to suit national and local level circumstances.

Remember to be flexible and creative and consider the economic, political, social, legal and cultural contexts of the country.

The Purpose of the Manual

The manual has been developed with a view to:

- introducing the integrated approach developed by the Commonwealth Secretariat;

- assisting governments, NGOs, community-based workers and other relevant facilitators implementing programmes to eradicate GBV;

- promoting the co-ordination, development and implementation of coherent policies and programmes by government departments, institutions, NGOs and civil society working to eliminate GBV;

- assisting governments and other stakeholders to use the integrated approach in developing multi-disciplinary plans of action and programmes to combat GBV;

- enlisting government support for NGOs working in the area of GBV, promoting the sharing of resources and experiences as well as the exchange of information;

- assisting institutions and other stakeholders experienced in women's issues with additional planning tools and strategies to address GBV;

- assisting organisations, institutions and individuals involved in developing training programmes to use the framework in order to promote and protect women's rights.

Remember, collective focussed action yields tangible results.

How the Manual is Organised

The manual is divided into five sections:

- **Section 1** contains a brief introduction and the background to GBV.

- **Section 2** provides information about the training manual and its purpose.

- **Section 3** provides the duration of the programme, the training approach, the overall goal and objectives of the programme. This section also presents each session by title, activity, objectives, outputs, method, timing and the materials needed. It provides step-by-step training.

- **Section 4** appears as a separate section known as *The Facilitator's Guide*. It contains facilitator's notes that can be given to participants as handouts.

- **Section 5** contains references.

Remember to follow the training process, focus on participatory approaches for delivering information and keep to your objectives.

Users of the Manual

This manual is intended for:

- institutions and organisations needing guidance in developing plans and programmes on GBV;

- facilitators at national and community levels;

- training programmes for trainers;

- specific stakeholder groups, including traditional healers, political, community and religious leaders;

- women in business who may be confronted by perpetrators;

- government departments involved in eradicating GBV;

- private sector institutions interested in supporting the eradication of GBV;

- NGOs working in the area of GBV;

- indigenous groups affected by the problem and motivated to take action against it;

- women and men as separate groups in the community;

- development workers whose work is related to the elimination of GBV.

Section 3

The Programme

Duration
The training programme is designed to last for a minimum of three days. However, it can be reviewed and extended to five days; depending on the national context and available resources.

Participants
For national level workshops, participants are drawn from government ministries, strategic departments, NGOs, intergovernmental organisations, multilateral agencies, relevant institutions, as well as other critical groups that support women's rights issues.

Participants at other levels of consultation will depend on government departments and organisations including NGOs and community groups in that area. The number of participants will depend on the resources available. However, a manageable number is between 30 and 40.

Remember, an overloaded programme compressed into limited time, will not produce quality results, likewise a scanty, unfocussed programme is not useful. Plan the workshop carefully and aim for results.

Training Approach
The manual suggests the use of highly participatory approaches in delivering the programme which:

- recognises the central role of the learners;
- takes into account and respects the fact that learners too have expertise, talents, experiences of their own and should be given scope for expression;
- acknowledges the self-esteem of groups and recognises that they have creative and analytical capacity, to identify and solve their own problems;
- draws on the associative strengths and resourcefulness of all stakeholders interested in the process, encourages collective action and planning, and promotes responsibility for joint action.

The manual therefore suggests some participatory methods such as case-studies, critical incidents, visual presentations, extracts from relevant studies and other participatory methods.

Facilitators are free to be creative in their participatory approaches, by drawing on the experiences of other countries in the region, and their own creative methods.

Remember, do not give long lectures, involve the participants; it is their workshop.

The Overall Goal and Objectives of the Programme
The overall goal of the programme is to assist stakeholders in respective countries to develop a plan of action that will enable them to work in a collaborative and co-ordinated manner to address the issue of GBV.

Specifically the programme aims at:

- building a consensus on the concept of GBV;

- deepening the participants' understanding of the extent, nature, causes, consequences and concept of GBV;

- defining and analysing the national and international legal frameworks, within which GBV is being addressed including policy, legal and other administrative arrangements at the national, provincial and community levels;

- sharing experiences in implementing different programmes to address GBV and assessing the status of these interventions;

- defining and analysing the social, cultural, economic and legal context in which the victims and perpetrators of GBV live;

- developing an understanding of an integrated approach to GBV, and analysing the steps necessary to ensure the involvement of all state and non-state stakeholders;

- equipping trainers with the relevant skills for developing a plan of action, and implementing an integrated approach to addressing GBV;

- assisting participants to develop their own plans of action;

- developing facilitation skills for introducing an integrated approach to combat GBV.

Remember not to lose sight of the major goal and objectives. Stay focussed.

Planning and Organising the Workshop

The estimated planning time is at least one month before the workshop. You will need about three days of planning with the national facilitators and organisers. The workshop should be organised in collaboration with the lead agency. This could be the Ministry responsible for Women/Gender Affairs for national workshops, or a commissioning agency at the local level.

Planning and organising involves:

Financial Arrangements
- preparing a budget for the workshop and administering it.

Organising Support and Agreeing on Tasks
- setting up a workshop committee;

- identifying, inviting and briefing resource persons about their tasks.

Stakeholder Enrolment and Involvement
- preparing the programme in consultation with the workshop organising committee and resource persons;

- preparing terms of reference for resource persons and rapporteurs, as well as presentations by stakeholders on work undertaken by their organisations in the area GBV;

- identifying resource persons and rapporteurs;

- identifying key stakeholders, organisations and individuals;

- identifying a suitable venue and arranging other logistics such as transportation, accommodation, meals, equipment and other welfare and administrative issues.

Protocol
- selecting and inviting workshop participants and guests to the official opening and any other related functions;
- identifying the guest of honour or keynote speaker and preparing speeches;
- inviting key in-country bilateral and multilateral agencies, and regional and international agencies that support gender programmes, to the official opening ceremony. These can include organisations such as UNDP, UNICEF, SIDA, CIDA, NORAD, DANIDA, British Council, World Bank, among others;
- researching, liaising and advising on the aspects that should inform the keynote address and other related protocol issues:
- ensuring that a director of ceremonies who is knowledgeable about GBV issues and who is sensitive to protocol can be identified. The director of ceremonies can be from within, or outside government.

Ensure that the keynote address is delivered at the highest political level to demonstrate the country's commitment to eliminating GBV.

Other Logistics
- preparing workshop training materials, folders, registration and evaluation forms;
- publicising the workshop through print and electronic media;
- preparing the training room so that it can be conducive to learning;
- liaising with the media to set everything up in good time;
- alerting all the speakers in advance,briefing them thoroughly and providing them with guidelines.

Remember if you fail to plan, you plan to fail.

Session 1: Setting the Scene

Overall Objective
To set the scene and make participants aware of the general issues relating to GBV and the need for national commitment to eradicate the problem.

This session consists of the following three activities:

- Opening ceremony
- Introductions
- Expectations, constraints, overall goal and objectives

Activity 1	
Opening ceremony	
Objective	• To aim the workshop at the highest possible political and official level.
Output	• Awareness of GBV issues among politicians, senior officials and other critical stakeholders; • Government and other stakeholders' commitment to eradicate GBV.
Timing	45 minutes
Method	• Delivery of keynote address and observance of associated issues of protocol.
Process	• Prepare the venue in advance for the official opening, identify ushers to meet the dignitaries and officials; • Different officials make their presentations and a plenary discussion ensues, involving questions, clarification, and comments; • Collect all speeches and papers.
Materials needed	Official opening programme and speeches.

Remember, official openings are important, but can also take up a great deal of time. Be in control.

Activity 2	
Introductions	
Objective	• To get participants to introduce themselves and the work of their organisations.
Output	• All participants introduced and a general appreciation of the organisations represented.
Timing	45 minutes
Method	• The facilitator is free to use any participatory method,(e.g. icebreakers or openers) that is relevant to the theme of the workshop. Use a creative icebreaker, such as the name-game, or a pairing exercise that will help participants to relax. This will result in a participatory learning environment.
Process	• Involve all the participants in the icebreakers, openers or games.
Materials needed	Notes on icebreakers, games and energisers. Refer to *The Facilitator's Guide* pages 79–81.

Remember to make the introductory session as interesting and exciting as possible.

Activity 3	
Expectations, constraints, overall goal and objectives.	
Objective	• To allow participants the opportunity to express their expectations and concerns, and reconcile these with the overall workshop goal and objectives.
Output	• A list of participants' expectations and concerns, which have been reconciled with the overall workshop goal and objectives.
Timing	30 minutes
Method	• Use of cards, brainstorming, and summaries.
Process	• Ask each participant to record on one card the most critical expectation, and on another card, the most critical constraint; • Collect the cards and categorise them under relevant headings such as awareness creation, capacity strengthening, service provision, resources etc; • Discuss the expectations and concerns. In plenary agree on their relevance and what can be realistically achieved during the workshop; • Post the categorised participants' expectations where they can be easily referred to throughout the workshop and for the final workshop evaluation; • Conclude this activity by relating the participants' expectations to the overall goal and objectives of the workshop.
Materials needed	Different coloured cards, markers, flipchart.

Remember, it is their workshop. Give them an opportunity to express their feelings, fears and concerns.

Session 2: The Concept, Extent, Nature, Causes, Consequences and Definition of Gender-Based Violence

Overall Objectives

To deepen participants' understanding of the concept, extent, nature, causes, consequences and definition of GBV.

This session consists of three activities:

- The concept of GBV

- The extent, nature, causes, consequences and definition of GBV

- Victims and perpetrators

Activity 1	
The concept of gender-based violence	
Objectives	• To solicit views from the participants on their understanding of violence in general and of the concept of GBV in particular; • To assist participants to generate factors that form the concept of GBV.
Output	• A checklist of factors that relate to the concept of GBV; • An agreed concept of GBV.
Timing	1 hour
Method	• Group discussion, brainstorming and the mind-mapping technique; • The probing technique.

Process	• Brainstorm the factors that can lead to GBV;
	
	• Facilitate a report-back session and record responses;
	Use the guiding questions listed below:
	
	  ♦ What comes to your mind when you think about violence?
	
	  ♦ What factors can lead to violence?
	
	  ♦ How do women and men perceive violence?
	
	  ♦ How do women and men react to violence?
	
	• Divide the participants into groups.
	Assign each group a factor to analyse, using the following questions:
	
	  ♦ What forms of violence are related to this factor and where are they likely to occur?
	
	  ♦ How does each form affect women and men, girls and boys?
	
	  ♦ Which of these forms of violence are gender-motivated, that is to say those that are suffered by women because they are women, and those that are suffered by men because they are men?
	
	• Facilitate report back on the discussions and presentations;
	
	• Consolidate the key emerging issues from the groups;
	
	• Agree on and record the agreed concept of GBV.

Activity 2

The extent, nature, causes, consequences and definition of gender-based violence

	• To find out from participants to what extent GBV occurs, the types of GBV they know about, and that exist in their communities; • To give participants an opportunity to discuss and agree on the deep-rooted causes and consequences of GBV; • To give participants an opportunity to discuss and agree on the definition of GBV.
	• An agreed checklist of the types of GBV; • Key points on the extent of its occurrence; • Key points on the nature of GBV; • Key points on the root causes and consequences of gender-based violence; • A working definition of GBV.
	2 ¹/₂ hours
	• Group discussions with guiding questions on the extent, nature, causes, consequences and definition of GBV; • Use of probing techniques, and the "But Why?" method; • Reinforcing knowledge and restating key points.

	• Divide participants into two groups with each group discussing any one of the following sub-topics;
	    • the extent and nature of GBV;
	    • the cause and consequences of GBV.
	• Facilitate a report-back session through group presentations.
	• Allow the largest group to ask questions and provide suggestions to involve all participants.
	• Record new information and ideas generated by the larger group.
	• Summarise and present key points on a transparency or flipchart.
	• Use the guiding questions below for each key issue.
	
	Guiding Questions
	
	Group 1: Questions on the nature and extent of GBV:
	• What are the characteristics or the extent of GBV?
	• How widespread is each of the listed forms/types?
	• What types of GBV do you know about?
	• What can be done to strengthen the current efforts to understand the extent and nature of GBV?
	
	Group 2: Questions on the causes and consequences of GBV:
	• What are the deep-rooted causes of GBV?
	• Why does GBV exist in our communities?
	• What are the consequences of GBV, and whom do these consequences impact on most?
	• What can be done to strengthen the current efforts to understand the causes and consequences of GBV?
	
	GBV is suffered by both women and men. Probe deeper to establish the various forms that are perpetuated by women and men.
	Draw from group reports in summarising the extent, nature, causes, and consequences of GBV.
	Arrive at a group GBV definition, drawing from group discussions and the facilitator's notes.

The definition of GBV

- Engage the participants in a mind-mapping exercise to reach a consensus on the definition of GBV.

- What words are associated with GBV?

- Write the words beside the mind-mapping circle, using arrows.

- Ask participants to divide into groups and come up with a working definition.

- Agree on a working definition.

Activity 3	
Victims and Perpetrators of GBV	
Objectives	• To discover who can be affected most by GBV, and why? • To discover who the perpetrators are, and why they commit such violent acts.
Output	• A checklist of those individuals most affected by GBV in order of the degree of impact; • Reasons why they are the most affected; • A checklist of the perpetrators and the reasons for committing such violent acts.
Timing	1 hour
Method	• Use of critical incident.
Process	• Divide the participants into groups; • Distribute the critical incident paper to each group; • Allow 20 minutes for discussion and facilitate a group report-back; • Agree on which individuals are the most affected and why this is the case; • Agree on the perpetrators and why they commit such violent acts; The critical incident relating to this activity can be found in *The Facilitator's Guide*, page 82. Present the key points stated below as a summary, either at the end of each activity or session as appropriate.
Materials needed	Guiding questions, markers, flipcharts, transparencies, handouts and critical incidents, and illustrations under mind-mapping techniques in *The Facilitator's Guide*, page 80.

- GBV is grossly under reported. It mostly occurs in private. The extent of GBV is therefore unknown. The methods of collecting data are not consistent, and some victims are reluctant to talk about the problem and report acts of violence.

- GBV involves a violation of human rights that results in all forms of violence based on gender relations. It is clearly linked to economic, political, and socio-cultural factors. Efforts to combat GBV lack adequate support from formal and informal structures and mechanisms.

- GBV includes physical acts, sexual harm, emotional/psychological abuse, economic deprivation and negative cultural practices. It occurs at different levels, that is in the home, the community, the workplace, in various institutions, and at the state level.

- Although the exact causes are not known, some of them include women's subordinate position, low social and economic status, negative cultural norms, values and practices. Other factors include the lack of communication and consultation in the home, the lack of power sharing between women and men, high poverty levels and conflict situations.

- GBV has numerous consequences for the individual victim, the family, the community and the state. These include, injury, disability, depression, isolation, low self-esteem, lack of confidence, low productivity levels, HIV/AIDS, mental disability, divorce and even death.

- The economic costs of GBV are enormous and impact on national development. Costs include; loss of working hours and the expenses for the provision of social, legal, and other facilities by the state.

- GBV is understood differently by various individuals, depending on their field of work, the country they come from, or the community they belong to. While there is no consensus on how to define it, that it exists is accepted all over the world.

- Within the different group definitions, there are areas where all groups agree on certain actions that constitute GBV. Therefore, there may be areas of intersection, where some of the groups agree, and some do not. It is only after negotiation of a common understanding and reaching an agreement on the different aspects of GBV that a working definition to address GBV can be formulated.

- GBV is a social problem and a development issue that should be addressed by governments, civil society, the media, and development agencies.

- GBV affects women, men and children as individuals in families, communities and the state. However, women and girls are disproportionately affected. This is because they are the majority of victims. The following aspects worsen the levels of violence against women:

  - armed conflict, the feminisation of poverty, the adverse impact of structural adjustment programmes (SAPs);

  - HIV/AIDS, and cross country trafficking in women;

  - social, cultural, economic and political realities in different regions;

  - low levels of literacy in women;

  - limited participation of women in decision-making positions;

  - discriminatory customary practices which have made women more vulnerable.

- The majority of perpetrators are men who may be strangers, acquaintances or family members, including husband and partners. There are various reasons why the perpetrators commit such acts of violence. Some of these are:

  - the power that men have over women, or are supposed to have;

  - inadequate or non-existent laws to address GBV;

  - the fact that men are not able to release their emotions to unburden themselves;

  - the lack of stringent law enforcement mechanisms;

  - untrained law enforcement officers and other legal practitioners in GBV interventions.

- We know very little about the nature and extent of GBV. The causes are multiple and deep rooted. The consequences are not fully understood. Until we do something about this situation, we shall be limited in our strategies. But the starting point is negotiation, so that we expand the concept of GBV beyond our own individual or group context.

Session 3: The Legal Framework

Overall Objective
To highlight the legal and policy framework at the national, regional and international levels, as well as to support mechanisms which address GBV at all levels.

The session consists of the following activities:

- National legal framework and challenges

- National and community level mechanisms and support services for accessing justice

- International standards and mechanisms

- Exercises and analysis of case studies, critical incidents and key informant views on gender-based violence

Activity 1	
The national legal framework	
Objectives	• To analyse national policies and laws relating to GBV; • To discuss the limitations and agree on how the policies and laws can be strengthened to eliminate GBV.
Output	• Participants' awareness of national laws and policies, as well as their limitations for addressing GBV; • A list of laws and policies that address GBV; • Recommendations for improving laws and policies on GBV.
Timing	1 hour
Method	• Brainstorming, questioning, and plenary discussion.
Process	• In plenary, ask participants to explain the laws and policies that address GBV, and list them; • Ask why they think these laws are related to GBV; • Brainstorm the limitations of these laws and policies and record them. Ask participants to suggest how these laws and policies can be improved; • Allow the resource person to give an overview of the national legal and policy framework, covering key issues raised by participants and her/his specific recommendations to fill in the gaps.
Materials needed	Flipchart, markers, transparencies and handouts

Present the key points stated below as a summary.

- Some countries have specific gender and/or women in development policies that call for equal participation, equity and equality for all women and men in the development process. However, many of those policies do not explicitly cover GBV as a social and development problem, which requires clear policies and strategies to guide the various interventions. This is compounded by the lack of a clear definition of what constitutes GBV as well as national plans to address the problem.

- Most countries have well-established provisions on equality, non-discrimination and the protection of women's rights. These provide a legal framework within which GBV can be addressed. Human rights provisions include the right to life, the right to development, freedom from torture, inhuman and degrading treatment.

- Other provisions include:

  - criminal laws which address murder, assault, battery and sexual offences;

  - civil laws which address assault, cruelty and evolving crimes, such as sexual harassment at the workplace;

  - procedural laws which are rules to facilitate the application of the law;

  - policies that are frameworks within which the laws are implemented.

- The effectiveness of these provisions in addressing GBV is hampered by the fact that the implementing structures are highly male-dominated. Decisions taken are influenced by male values and attitudes. There is also no guarantee that female law enforcement officers are gender-sensitive.

- It should be recognised that many people, women and men, are not familiar with the national legal framework. In some instances, especially in rural areas, many people resort to the use of non-formal means of resolving conflicts, through interventions managed by community courts, community leaders, chiefs, and politicians, among others.

Activity 2	
Mechanisms and support systems for accessing justice at national and local levels	
Objectives	• To increase the participants' awareness of formal and non-formal legal mechanisms and support systems at national and community levels that address GBV; • To identify the strengths and weaknesses of the formal and non-formal legal mechanisms and support systems, and make recommendations for improving access to justice.
Output	• A common understanding of existing formal and non-formal mechanisms and support systems, at national and local levels, their strengths and weaknesses; • Recommendations for improving access to justice by women and men, including suggestions for more focussed mechanisms and support systems.
Timing	1 hour
Method	• Brainstorming, group work and summaries.
Process	• In plenary, ask participants to identify the formal and non-formal legal systems, used at national and community levels, including formal courts, community courts and any other mechanisms of dispute resolution at local level; • Record responses under two headings: formal and non-formal legal systems; • In groups, ask participants to discuss the strengths and weaknesses of each system, and suggest recommendations for improving access to justice by the victims of GBV; • In plenary, participants report back, discuss responses as well as recommendations and record key issues that emerge; • Allow the resource person or experts working in the legal area to fill in the gaps; • Collect new information from the resource person and prepare a handout; • Summaries can also draw on key points from those raised in the discussion group.

Activity 3	
International instruments and mechanisms	
Objective	• To deepen participants' understanding of the international instruments, relevant to GBV, their benefits, limitations and how they can be used to influence national and local level strategies.
Output	• Increased understanding of the international instruments, the benefits and limitations and how they can be used to influence national efforts to combat GBV.
Timing	1 $\frac{1}{2}$ hours
Method	• Mind-mapping, exercise and brainstorming techniques.

Process	• Draw an illustration or a big circle on a flipchart, insert the topic or issue you are addressing in the middle of the illustration, or, ask the following question:
	
	  ◆ What international instruments do you know of which are related to GBV? Discuss the responses.
	
	• Then ask the following questions:
	
	  ◆ What are the limitations of international instruments?
	
	  ◆ How can international instruments be used to influence national action to address GBV?
	
	• Discuss the responses in plenary and record the key issues?
	
	• Allow the resource person to give an overview of the international instruments relevant to GBV and allow participants to ask questions; encourage note taking.
	
	• Present the key points stated below as a summary.

Materials needed	Illustrations, markers, flipchart, and handouts.

The international community has always developed frameworks such as declarations, conventions, treaties and other instruments, to address particular needs which call for international attention. For example, Universal Declaration of Human Rights, CEDAW, The Inter-American Convention on Prevention and Eradication of Violence Against Women, European Convention on Human Rights, African Charter on Human and People's Rights, The UN Declaration on the Elimination of Violence Against Women, and the SADC Gender and Development and Declaration and its Addendum on Prevention and Eradication of Violence Against Women and Children.

Although these instruments are not automatically binding, they provide a framework within which to deal with the problem of GBV in the different countries. Most countries have signed and ratified these international instruments, and have even incorporated some of the principles into their national constitutions and laws. However, countries that have signed, ratified and incorporated these instruments into their laws, policies and programmes should ensure that these measures are gender responsive. This will go a long way to address the specific needs of women and men, reduce GBV and improve their lives.

The limitations of implementing these frameworks include, among others, the following:

- Many countries have enacted laws and some have not done so;

- Some states have signed, but expressed reservations about some of the articles;

- Many policymakers, legislators, women and men, as well as law enforcement officers, are not aware of the content of these laws;

- Countries are not bound to implement, they are only bound to report.

Activity 4	
Exercises and analysis of case studies, critical incidents and key informant views on gender-based violence	
Objectives	• To examine the participants' understanding of the legal framework, mechanisms and support systems; • To examine the inherent limitations and critical actions needed to improve access to justice for women and men who suffer GBV.
Output	• The ability to demonstrate their awareness of the existing legal framework, mechanisms and support systems relevant to specific incidents and forms of GBV.
Timing	1 hour
Method	Group work, report-back, discussions and presentation of a short summary.
Process	• Divide the participants into groups; • Distribute case studies, critical incidents and key informant views to the groups; • Ask the participants in their groups to discuss and analyse the case studies etc; • Facilitate a report-back session; • Agree on mechanisms and support systems necessary to redress the issues; • Record key issues raised by participants; • The case studies, critical incidents and key informant views and the relevant questions are in *The Facilitator's Guide* pages 82–84. Photocopy these in advance.
Materials needed	Copies of case studies, critical incidents, key informant views, transparencies, markers and flipchart.

Present a summary of the key issues stated below:

Each country has adopted legal mechanisms and put in place support systems and institutional arrangements, to implement laws relating to GBV. These are:

- The criminal justice system, including the police who investigate, arrest and prosecute;

- The Department of Public Prosecutions (DPP);

- Social welfare/probation which handles complaints relating to family matters, and provides counselling services;

- The judiciary which involves courts at all levels in the adjudication of cases;

- The Ministry of Legal Affairs/Justice responsible for the overall administration of the law;

- The Health Department which treats both victims and perpetrators; forensic scientists;

- Institutions that carry out research on GBV;

- NGOs who are involved in providing legal aid, legal education, research, advocacy and other facilities;

- Informal structures and mechanisms including community courts conducted by traditional leaders (chiefs, elders and politicians);

- Clan and tribal conflict resolution settings at family level and by peer groups.

Session 4: Sharing Experiences and Challenges

Overall Objectives
To give participants an opportunity to share experiences and challenges as organisations dealing with combating GBV, and to help them to reach a common understanding on the benefits of collective action.

This session consists of three activities:

- Taking stock of current activities/interventions

- The stakeholder development scenario

- Challenges of collective action by organisations working in the area of GBV

Activity 1	
Taking stock of current activities	
Objectives	• To give participants an opportunity to share experiences of activities undertaken in the area of GBV; • To allow participants to share lessons learnt in the area of GBV; • To give participants an opportunity to discuss and agree on the ways in which they can work together to eradicate GBV.
Output	• Shared experiences of activities/interventions in the area of GBV; • Lessons learnt; • A checklist of solutions generated.
Timing	1 hour
Method	• Group work and plenary discussions.

Process	• Divide participants into four groups. Each group discusses one of the following topics:
	
	  ♦ activities relating to GBV implemented by their organisations;
	
	  ♦ lessons learnt;
	
	  ♦ recommendations/challenges in terms of building result-orientated relationship.
	
	• Allow time for groups to discuss the topics assigned to them.
	
	• Distribute the following discussion points to guide the group discussion:
	
	  ♦ In your groups discuss the activities or interventions you undertake in your organisations/institutions that address GBV.
	
	  ♦ Identify the areas of co-operation, co-ordination or duplication.
	
	  ♦ What lessons have you learnt as organisations working together on issues of GBV?
	
	  ♦ How can you improve co-operation and collaboration?
	
	• Facilitate a report-back session through group presentation;
	
	• Allow for plenary discussion and contributions from the largest group;
	
	• Record the key emerging issues and incorporate new ideas from the largest group.

Materials needed	Handouts on discussion points, flipchart and markers.

Activity 2

The stakeholder development scenario

Objectives	<ul><li>To give participants an opportunity to analyse the critical stakeholders in the area of GBV at the national and local level;</li><li>To allow participants to identify the challenges of a stakeholder enrolment and involvement scenario;</li><li>To encourage participants to generate solutions on the best strategies for stakeholder development.</li></ul>
Output	<ul><li>A list of critical stakeholders in GBV;</li><li>A checklist of challenges related to stakeholder enrolment and involvement;</li><li>A checklist of possible solutions.</li></ul>
Timing	30 minutes
Method	<ul><li>Brainstorming and using the 'But Why?' method.</li></ul>
Process	<ul><li>Using the brainstorming technique, ask participants to generate a list of critical stakeholders within and outside government in the area of GBV;</li><li>Ask for justification of the list generated, such as why these stakeholders are critical;</li><li>Record the list of critical stakeholders and post it on the wall for future reference.</li></ul>
Materials needed	Flipchart, markers, masking tape, handouts and papers prepared by the different organisations

Activity 3	
Challenges for collective action for organisations working in the area of gender-based violence	
Objectives	• To solicit views from participants about the inherent challenges of successful collective action in the area of GBV; • To get the views of participants on how collective action in the area of GBV can be enhanced.
Output	• A checklist of challenges for successful collective action in the area of GBV; • A checklist of effective collective action.
Timing	30 minutes
Method	Group work and plenary discussion

Process	• Divide the participants into groups:
	
	• Distribute the following questions for discussion:
	
	   • What are the challenges for successful collective action by organisations working in the area of GBV?
	
	   • How can this collective action be enhanced?
	
	• Facilitate a report-back session through discussion and presentations;
	
	• Allow for plenary discussion;
	
	• Record the key points that emerge.

Materials needed	Flipchart, markers, masking tape, handout on guiding questions for activity sub-topics.

Present the following key points as a summary:

● A number of organisations and institutions, government departments, development partners, NGOs, CBOs and community groups work in the area of GBV.

● It is critical that the organisations leading in the area of GBV identify and analyse the critical stakeholders committed and dedicated to combating GBV.

● However, a number of challenges exist in holding these critical stakeholders together for collective action. Some of these challenges are:

   ◆ difficulty in bringing on board the relevant government ministries and departments such as the Ministries of Finance, Planning, Defence, Public Service, Education and other human rights institutions so that they play an active role in addressing GBV;

   ◆ lack of financial/human resources including a limited capacity for fundraising initiatives;

   ◆ inadequate government support for GBV programmes and projects;

   ◆ the lack of full recognition of NGOs and civil society by governments as complementary partners in development;

- the lack of recognition and encouragement by government for the effective participation of the private sector in efforts to combat GBV;

- the fear of loss of identity, which undermines efforts for collaboration and collective action, often expressed by NGOs.

- the lack of sharing of financial and human resources amongst NGOs and how to avoid duplicating efforts;

- the lack of diverse skills and capacity among stakeholders, including expertise in the area of networking, financial sustainability, effective management, practice, service delivery and good governance.

For the integrated approach to combating GBV to succeed, there is a need for all the critical stakeholders to act collectively through collaboration, co-ordination and effective networking.

Session 5: The Framework for Addressing GBV

Overall Objective
To discuss frameworks for combating GBV.

The major component activities of this session are:

- Introduction of the Commonwealth Gender Management Systems (GMS)

- Application of GMS principles for combating GBV

- Introduction of the Commonwealth model framework for an integrated approach to combat violence against women

- Application of the principles of the model framework to address GBV

Activity 1	
General Management Systems (GMS)	
Objective	• To highlight the principles of GMS. What it is, who can use it, its mission, goal and objectives, its stakeholder approach, and essential elements.
Output	• A basic understanding of the GMS approach to gender mainstreaming.
Timing	45 minutes
Method	The jigsaw puzzle, treasure hunt and presentation in plenary.

Process	• Present the GMS framework on a transparency;
	
	• Allow for an open discussion with guiding questions to develop the participants' understanding of GMS;
	
	• Facilitate an activity on stakeholder enrolment and involvement. The jigsaw puzzle is a good exercise to use here.
	
	• Give each group a numbered piece of the poster and allow participants to discuss their piece, using the following guiding questions:
	
	   • What is the shape, colour and characteristics of your piece?
	   • What does that mean to you as a stakeholder of GBV interventions?
	   • Can your organisation work alone to eliminate GBV?
	   • What is the right approach to take?
	   • What challenges do you face?
	   • What are the key learning points for you as stakeholders?
	
	• Record participants' responses.
	
	• Conclude this activity by drawing on the handout on GMS and the facilitator's notes. To increase participants' involvement, use any method, e.g. the treasure hunt or the mixed bag, using the guiding questions above. Feel free to elaborate on the questions, or formulate new ones based on issues emerging from the discussion.
	
	• Ask participants to put together their puzzle pieces in order to reconstruct the complete poster. Then ask the following questions:
	
	   • What is GMS?
	   • Who can use it?
	   • What is the GMS mission?
	   • What are the objectives of GMS?
	   • What is the GMS stakeholder approach?
	   • What are the essential elements of a GMS system?
	   • Ask different participants to pick cards/pieces of paper and read the question. Ask them to provide the initial response or ask other participants to do so.
	
	Use the GMS summary in *The Facilitator's Guide*, page 61.

Materials needed	Handouts, transparencies, markers, flipchart, manila card, and posters

While summarising this activity, make a direct application of the GMS principles to the efforts to combat GBV. The following checklist will be useful in focusing this summary:

- How can the GMS framework assist government and non-state individuals to implement plans of action and strategies for combating GBV?

- What strengths would the framework collectively bring to stakeholders?

- What are the indicators for effective action in addressing GBV through the following;

  - an enabling environment? (political will, adequate human and financial resources policy, legislative and administrative frameworks, women in decision-making positions at all levels, active involvement of civil society)

  - a clear process? (well-defined structures and mechanisms, an agreed plan of action, recognition of the need for, and inclusion of, a gender dimension)

  - structures? (lead agency, management team, focal points and steering committee)

  - mechanisms? (gender-sensitisation, analysis and planning, training, management information systems, and localised eradication of GBV)

Remember, giving participants the opportunity to ask questions. Restating the various principles and objectives in their own words can clear up misunderstandings.

Activity 2

The Commonwealth model framework for an integrated approach to combat violence against women

Objective	• To introduce the Commonwealth model framework for the integrated approach to combat violence against women and apply its principles to eliminating GBV.
Output	• An understanding of, and commitment to, an integrated approach; • A consensus reached on using the integrated approach.
Timing	$1\frac{1}{2}$ hours
Method	Introduction, group discussions and summary.

Process	• Present the following key points as an introduction:
	
	   ◆ Many state and non-state individuals or organisations are doing related work, and yet they continue to work in isolation;
	
	   ◆ It is difficult to accurately determine overall national efforts to combat GBV, because of poor reporting and lack of accountable structures;
	
	   ◆ Targets are more often confined to organisations with little co-ordination at national level.
	
	   ◆ In the light of this, the Commonwealth Secretariat has developed a model framework for an integrated approach to combat violence against women.
	
	• Divide the participants into 4-6 groups;
	
	• Explain the following guiding questions:
	
	   ◆ What do you understand by an integrated approach to GBV?
	
	   ◆ Why do we need an integrated approach and what benefits can we derive from adopting such an approach?
	
	   ◆ Who are the stakeholders who should be involved in implementing the integrated approach?
	
	   ◆ What factors can reduce the impact of the integrated approach?
	
	   ◆ What are the critical success factors needed to make an integrated approach work?
	
	• Allow time for discussion;
	
	• Facilitate the report-back and record all the key points raised by participants.

Materials needed	Transparencies, markers, flipchart, handouts

Present a summary focussing on the following using slides 1–4 in *The Facilitator's Guide*, pages 66–73:

- Why the integrated approach?
- The advantages of the integrated approach;
- The Commonwealth model framework for an integrated approach to combat violence against women, and its key elements (conceptualisation and a deeper understanding of the problem, actions and strategies as well as co-ordination mechanisms and assumptions of the model framework). Refer to page 69 in *The Facilitator's Guide*.

Activity 3

Analysing the application of the Commonwealth model framework to the national context

Objective	• To get the participants to analyse the Commonwealth integrated model framework and reach a consensus on whether such a framework will be applicable to their situation.
Output	• Analysis of the framework; • A list of challenges likely to be faced in implementing the framework; • Critical success factors for a workable integrated approach; • Identification of relevant structures to implement the model framework; • Consensus reached on using the framework and acceptance of the framework.
Timing	• 1½ hours
Method	• Group work using the following guiding questions: ◆ What factors can facilitate the application of the model in your country? ◆ What structures need to be established in order to make the integrated approach work? ◆ Which body is competent to co-ordinate? ◆ What should its composition and mandate be? Give reasons for your responses; ◆ Who should be responsible for instituting the co-ordination mechanisms?
Process	• Divide the participants into groups and explain the guiding questions above; • Listen to group discussions and advise as necessary; • Facilitate the report-back and record issues emerging from group reports; Reach a consensus on the key issues.
Materials needed	Flipchart and markers, handouts, guiding questions, transparencies, the Commonwealth model framework for an integrated approach for combating violence against women, GMS and mind map

- Present a summary focussing on the following key points:

  ◆ Why will the integrated approach work?

  ◆ What challenges are likely to be faced and how can these be solved?

  ◆ What relevant structures and mechanisms are necessary for implementing the integrated approach, including the different roles and responsibilities for the various stakeholders?

  ◆ Which body should be responsible for instituting the co-ordination mechanisms?

If we support the victims and survivors of gender-based violence, as well as the perpetrators, using an integrated approach we can significantly reduce the incidence of this scourge.

Session 6: Developing the Plan of Action

Overall Objective
To help participants prepare a plan of action for implementing an integrated approach to combat GBV.

This session consist of four activities:

- Key areas for developing the plan of action
- Defining the terms
- Logical steps for developing the plan of action
- Developing the plan of action

Activity 1	
Key areas for developing the plan of action	
Objective	• To enable the participants to generate key areas that will guide them in developing the plan of action.
Output	• An understanding of key areas for the plan of action.
Timing	• 45 minutes
Method	• Use of the checklist of key areas and brainstorming.

Process	• Divide the participants into groups.
	
	• Distribute the following checklist:
	
	  ◆ Deepening the understanding of the extent, nature, causes and consequences and concept of GBV;
	
	  ◆ Identifying the needs, support systems, and services for victims, survivors and perpetrators;
	
	  ◆ Understanding international, regional and national legal frameworks, mechanisms and support systems for combating GBV;
	
	  ◆ The stakeholder development scenario;
	
	  ◆ The integrated approach to combating GBV and Gender Management Systems (GSM)
	
	  ◆ Capacity building for GBV stakeholders to enhance leadership, management, co-ordination and collaboration;
	
	  ◆ Allocating roles and responsibilities to different stakeholders and monitoring relevant structures that support GBV.
	
	• Ask the participants to analyse and validate the checklist.
	
	• Participants can add other areas which they consider critical for the plan of action.
	
	• Allow 20 minutes for group discussion.
	
	• Facilitate the report-back.
	
	• Record issues emerging from the group reports.
	
	• Help participants to prioritise the key areas.

Materials needed	Checklist of key areas, flipchart, markers, handouts

A deeper understanding of gender-based violence will motivate us to formulate focussed objectives, workable strategies, implementable activities, measurable indicators and timely action within the available resources.

Activity 2	
Defining the terms	
Objective	• To define the standard terms which are the core components of the plan of action.
Output	• Understanding of the standard terms that constitute the core plan of action.
Timing	30 minutes
Method	Mind-mapping, group work and plenary discussion

Process	• Engage the participants in a mind-mapping exercise to create an understanding of the strategy and objectives of a plan;
	• Presenting one term at a time, engage the participants in a brainstorming session, using the following questions as triggers:
	    ◆ What words, phrases or sentences are associated with the strategy and objectives?
	    ◆ Define the strategy and objectives using the words and phrases that you have generated;
	    ◆ Give an example in each case;
	    ◆ Record the key points;
	    ◆ Post the information where participants can see it;
	• Divide the participants into seven groups to answer questions on: activities, target group, time-frame, resources, lead agency, funding agency, and risks and assumptions.
	
	Guiding questions for group work:
	
	Group 1: Activity
	    ◆ How would you define an activity?
	    ◆ What activities are related to GBV?
	    ◆ Under what broad topics would the activities that you have listed fall?
	    ◆ What critical factors should you consider when determining activities?
	
	Group 2: Target Group
	    ◆ How would you define a target group?
	    ◆ What are the target groups that should benefit from, and contribute towards, efforts to combat GBV?
	    ◆ What are the advantages of focussing action on addressing the needs of these GBV target groups?
	    ◆ What are the disadvantages of not doing so?
	
	Group 3: Time-frame
	    ◆ What do you understand by time-frame in relation to any plan?
	    ◆ Why are time-frames important?
	    ◆ What are the features of a time-frame, or how do you determine a time-frame?

Group 4: Resources

- ◆ What is your general understanding of resources?
- ◆ What do you understand by resources in the context of GBV?
- ◆ What skills do you need to mobilise resources?
- ◆ Do these skills exist within the stakeholder groups?
- ◆ What strategies can you employ to be able to optimise and mobilise supplementary resources in an integrated manner?

Group 5: Lead Agency

- ◆ What are the characteristics of a lead agency?
- ◆ Which body do you think should co-ordinate the integrated approach to combating GBV? Give reasons for your response.
- ◆ What should the mandate of this body be?
- ◆ Suggest a capacity-building programme for the lead agency.
- ◆ Should there be a separate monitoring body? If so, what should its composition and mandate be?

Group 6: Funding Agency

- ◆ What agencies have supported women's human rights and GBV activities in the past?
- ◆ What are the expectations of these agencies?
- ◆ What skills are needed for successful fund-raising initiatives?
- ◆ How can we mobilise and rationalise resources?
- ◆ Who should take overall responsibility, particularly in dealing with donors?

Group 7: Risks and Assumptions

- ◆ What factors can contribute to the successful implementation of each activity?
- ◆ What factors can prevent the successful implementation of each activity?
- ◆ How can you ensure success and avoid the risks?
- ● Facilitate a report-back session and allow the largest group to ask questions and make comments.
- ● Consolidate key points from the various groups.
  - ◆ Present a summary of the discussion.

Materials needed	Flipchart, markers, and grid

A well thought out and focussed plan is easier to commit to, and should facilitate the elimination of gender-based violence.

Activity 3	
A step-by-step approach to developing the plan of action	
Objective	• To help participants to understand the logical steps involved in developing a plan of action.
Output	• An understanding of the logical steps.
Timing	45 minutes
Method	Presentation and plenary discussion
Process	• Present the following logical steps of the various components in developing a plan of action. Use the detailed notes for the presentation. These are provided in *The Facilitator's Guide*, page 74. *Step 1:* Formulating the overall strategy *Step 2:* Formulating the objective which should be linked to the overall strategy *Step 3:* Development of activities *Step 4:* Identifying the target group *Step 5:* Agreeing on the lead agency *Step 6:* Identifying the implementers of the programme *Step 7:* Mobilising resources *Step 8:* Identifying funding agencies *Step 9:* Indicating time-frames *Step 10:* Stating indicators *Step 11:* Risks and assumptions Divide the participants into groups and allocate the areas for the development of the action plan. • Intersperse the presentation with questions to check understanding; • Restate information to increase understanding; • Use the information generated by participants during the group discussions and add to the key issues.
Materials needed	Handouts

Activity 4	
Developing the plan of action	
Objective	• To give participants an opportunity to draft a plan of action.
Output	• A first draft plan of action.
Timing	8 hours
Method	Group work and plenary

Process	• Divide the participants into groups according to the key areas, as indicated below.
	
	Areas for the plan of action:
	
	    ◆ Deepening the understanding of the nature, extent, causes and consequences of GBV;
	    ◆ Identifying the needs and support systems/services relating to the victims and perpetrators;
	    ◆ Understanding international, regional and national legal frameworks in the area of GBV;
	    ◆ The stakeholder development scenario;
	    ◆ Adopting an integrated approach to combating GBV based on Gender Management Systems principles (GMS);
	    ◆ Capacity-building for GBV stakeholders – including those not actively involved;
	    ◆ Identifying and allocating roles and responsibilities to stakeholders and monitoring relevant structures to support GBV.
	
	• Post the key issue areas agreed upon on the flipchart to keep the participants focussed;
	• Allocate other facilitators to groups to provide guidance;
	• Allow two hours for the groups to draft the plan of action (2 hours);
	• Facilitate group reports and presentations;
	• Allow other participants to make contributions to the areas that they did not participate in (3 hours):
	• Select a representative committee to consolidate the draft plan (2 hours);
	• Allow for a final presentation and discussion of the consolidated draft plan of action (45 minutes).

Materials needed	Handouts

Summary

Logical steps for developing the plan of action:

- Formulate the overall strategy;

- Formulate the objectives linked to the overall strategy;

- Develop activities emanating from the overall strategy and objectives;

- Identify the target-group/the critical stakeholders;

- Agree on the lead agency and its mandate;

- Identify the implementers of the GBV programme;

- Agree on the monitoring mechanisms;

- Identify sources of funding and other resources; mobilise and allocate them;

- Identify funding and other forms of support interventions;

- Indicate the time-frame for programme implementation as an objective;

- State the indicators of success quantitatively and qualitatively.

Section 4: The Facilitator's Guide

About *The Facilitator's Guide*

The Facilitator's Guide provides detailed notes and reference materials for the facilitator. These notes can be used during preparation for the workshop and training.

The objectives of *The Facilitator's Guide* are to:

- provide relevant information for the different sessions and activities;
- assist in the preparation of summaries for each session in The Do it Yourself Manual;
- create a better understanding and appreciation of GBV and strategies to be adopted to eradicate it.

What Does *The Facilitator's Guide* Contain?

The Facilitator's Guide contains detailed notes on the following sessions which are in turn divided into activities:

Session 1
- Setting the scene

Session 2
- The concept of GBV;
- The extent, nature, causes, consequences, and definition of GBV.

Session 3
- The national legal framework, its benefits, limitations, and what can be done to improve the legal environment, mechanisms and support systems;
- The international legal framework, declarations, conventions and other international agreements, the benefits and limitations;
- Analysis of mechanisms and support systems through case studies, critical incidents and key informant views; what exists, the challenges and how the situation can be improved.

Session 4
- Sharing experiences and challenges, the current situation, the missing links and how improvements can be made.

Session 5
- Gender Management Systems (GMS) – its mission, goals, objectives, essential elements, process, structures, and stakeholder approach;
- The integrated approach – advantages and concepts of the model, attempts made by various organisations to implement it, and a definition.

Session 6
- The road map to developing a plan of action – the logical steps;
- Some participatory methods.

Session 7

- Evaluating workshop activities;

- References

Key Points to Consider

- Read the facilitator's notes thoroughly so that you understand all the sessions, and discover what GBV entails;

- Note the links between the sessions and the activities;

- Use simple language when acting as the facilitator;

- Consider the level and background of the participants;

- Follow the logical sequence of each session which includes:

  - the objective(s)

  - the output

  - the timing

  - methods

  - process and materials needed.

Remember, stick to your purpose to achieve results. Timing is essential; be in control and involve participants in the whole process at every stage.

Methods

- Your approach to training should be participatory.

- Some suggested methods can be found on pages 79–81.

- Be creative and devise your own methods too, but these should be relevant and simple in order to encourage participation in terms of:

  - self-esteem

  - associative strengths

  - resourcefulness

  - action planning

  - responsibility for joint action

Be a participatory trainer and not a dictator. Involve participants at every stage. Show, don't tell.

Session 1: Setting the Scene

A successful trainer has to set the scene for a conducive learning atmosphere, at the beginning of any training event. What does this entail? It involves advising the lead agency on the following aspects of organising the workshop and observing protocol:

- Invite all the relevant officials, critical stakeholders, one month in advance. Attach the workshop programme to the invitation.

- Invite all the official presenters two months in advance, including the keynote speaker.

- Prepare guidelines for the official presenters and brief them thoroughly. Attach the programme to the invitation.

- Brief the keynote speaker separately.

- Liaise with the media in advance in order to set up the equipment in good time.

- Ensure that a director of ceremonies is identified who is knowledgeable about GBV, and is sensitive to protocol, from within or outside government.

- Ensure that the training room is appropriately arranged for the official opening event.

- Ensure that the dignitaries are properly received and seated for the official opening session.

Introductions are an essential entry point, they ensure participatory learning and a relaxed learning atmosphere.

There is likely to be a degree of variation between the participants' expectations and the goal and objectives of the workshop. Providing an opportunity at the beginning of the workshop for negotiating and agreeing on what can be realistically achieved during the workshop, will promote greater compatibility and enhance results.

A successful trainer will always be guided by the knowledge gap of the participants and their responses to learning stimuli.

Remember, this workshop should be aimed at the highest possible political level to foster commitment and a positive response from government officials and other critical supporters.

Session 2: The Concept, Extent, Nature, Causes, Consequences and Definition of Gender-based Violence

The Concept Of GBV
The concept of GBV involves a violation of human rights that results in all forms of violence based on gender relations. It includes physical harm, sexual acts, emotional/psychological abuse and economic deprivation.

The Extent of GBV
The extent of GBV is difficult to assess because of the following reasons:

- variations in agreement of what constitutes GBV;

- the fact that GBV is under-reported;

- data is usually not based on widescale research. Data therefore becomes a poor indicator of the scale of violence,

- methods used to collect data are at times inconsistent and therefore its validity is questionable;

- as it occurs mostly in private, it becomes a hidden crime;

- in the case of family violence, law enforcement officers are often reluctant to intervene in what they normally view as a private matter;

- even where cases are reported, there is limited usable information as most of the institutions do not keep proper records;

- highlighting violence within families sometimes overshadows the violence committed in public by strangers, acquaintances, state officials, other professionals such as doctors and teachers, as well as traditional and spiritual healers;

- women often withhold information on GBV for reasons that include fear of further assaults, loss of family income where the breadwinner is imprisoned, divorce, or other reasons such as fear of violating cultural values and norms;

- self blame is another reason that deters women from dealing appropriately with the problem;

- women often make information available after years of assault, maintaining that they stay in abusive relationships for the sake of the children.

The Nature of GBV
GBV takes various forms, which can be categorised in the following ways.

- Physical violence which includes:

    - slapping, punching, grabbing, kicking, shaking, pushing, pulling hair, restraint, biting, use of force/threat/coercion to obtain sex, use of weapons against him or her, battery, murder, destroying her/his possessions;

    - sexual acts which include sodomy, rape (and marital rape), genital mutilation, sexual harassment, incest, defilement and sexual violence committed during war crimes.

- Emotional/Psychological violence which includes:

- shouting, ridicule and humiliation, denial of safe sex;

- denying women freedom of movement or of association, verbal insults and forced marriages.

- Economic deprivation which includes:

  - denying women access to employment, failure to provide for the family, denying women access to education and training, discriminating against women in employment situations, and refusal to pay maintenance by father/partner.

The Causes of GBV

The exact causes of GBV are not known, but include the following:

- inequalities and imbalanced power relations between women and men in society;

- structures with a complex set of values, norms, practices, customs and traditions, beliefs and practices rooted in patriarchy and gender inequality;

- the lack of prevention programmes targeting the perpetrator, the community and the state;

- an inadequate and unfriendly legal environment, lack of information and awareness relating to the legal framework, reluctance or delays of governments in reviewing and reforming laws;

- lack of stakeholder enrolment and involvement in issues of GBV;

- women's poverty, coupled with a lack of knowledge of their human rights;

- lack of knowledge of who the real perpetrators are, labelling all men as perpetrators, which will stifle the success of the integrated approach to combating GBV;

- people do not like to expose their family life to public scrutiny, and society tries to protect the family institution. Some women and men also believe in this negative societal value, which sustains GBV.

The Consequences of GBV

GBV can have the following consequences.

Physical effects which include:

- death of the victim;

- the risk of contracting HIV/AIDS infection;

- maiming, bruises, fractures;

- the death of the perpetrator if the victim retaliates;

- injuries and harm extended to children, relatives and neighbours caught in violent situations.

Psychological effects which include:

- anxiety, depression, fear, degradation, humiliation and insecurity, and suicidal tendencies

All these factors result in emotional trauma for women, children and families.

Social effects which include:

- feelings of incompetence, low self-esteem, and lack of self worth;

- children can be traumatised and are likely to suffer in the process;

- divorce is at times a necessary end, this affects the children emotionally and may also result in loss of income and property for the victim;

- women's movements are curtailed, enterprising and working women may lose their source of income;

- an increase in the number of street children reported to come from broken homes;

- forms of dress are sometimes determined by society and so the abuse is blamed on the victim;

- women are isolated from society and deterred from participating in public life;

- stigmatisation of the family, which is usually considered to be the victim's fault;

- dependency by women on social systems such as welfare packages, police, hospitals where personnel are not always helpful.

Economic effects which include:

- low levels of productivity from abused women;

- the leadership potential and capacity of women remains untapped;

- the cost of medical treatment for the family escalates and deprives them of a good standard of living;

- governments spend a large amount of money on support services such as police, prisons, the judiciary, probation, and community services.

For example, Canada reported spending 32 million dollars annually and Botswana reported 100 million pula a year.

Other consequences involve:

- denying women and girls the most fundamental of human rights: of liberty, integrity and dignity;

- limiting women's options, choices and behaviour;

- limiting women's participation and involvement in the community and in public life;

- pain and feelings of betrayal.

Who Does it Affect and Why?
- GBV affects women, men, children, the family, the community and the state.

- Women and girls are more likely to be affected because they are the main victims.

- The following aspects worsen the level of violence against women:

  - armed conflict, the feminisation of poverty, the adverse impact of structural adjustment programmes (SAPs) and cross country trafficking in women;

- social, cultural, economic and political realities in different countries and regions;
- low levels of literacy in women;
- limited participation of women in decision-making positions and processes;
- discriminatory customary practices which make women more vulnerable.

The Reasons Why Perpetrators Commit Violent Acts

The majority of perpetrators are men. These may be strangers, acquaintances, family members, including husbands and partners. There are various reasons why the perpetrators commit such acts of violence. These include:

- sexual inequality and control over women by men;
- inadequate laws or non-existent laws, as well as lack of stringent law enforcement mechanisms that address GBV, men are not able to release their emotions to unburden themselves;
- the lack of gender sensitisation and analysis skills by law enforcement officers and other legal practitioners in order to deal with GBV effectively;
- the socialisation process and cultural norms which encourage abuse of women by men, viewing it as acceptable behaviour;
- the lack of training in anger management, conflict and dispute resolution between individuals and family members;
- poor communication between partners and the family.

The Definition of GBV

GBV is a discriminatory act, which affects individuals, families, the community and the state in many negative ways. It includes sexual, physical, emotional/psychological and economic abuse because of gender relations. It occurs in public and in private.

Summary

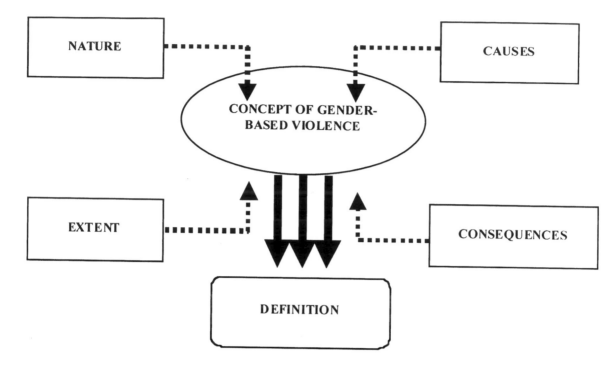

Notes:

- Participants' knowledge of the nature, causes, extent and consequences is key in facilitating the development of the concept of gender-based violence.

- This means that the more informed participants are about these four components, the richer their concept of gender-based violence. If they know little about any or all of these four building blocks, they are highly likely to have a weak and unbalanced concept of gender-based violence.

- Therefore, the level of participants' understanding of the nature, causes, extent and consequences has a direct proportional relationship with their ability to conceptualise gender-based violence.

- When participants understand the nature, causes, extent and consequences, they are likely to form a good concept of gender-based violence and therefore gain facility to define it in a comprehensive but clear manner.

Summary: Negotiation process for collective/group concept formation and definition of gender-based violence

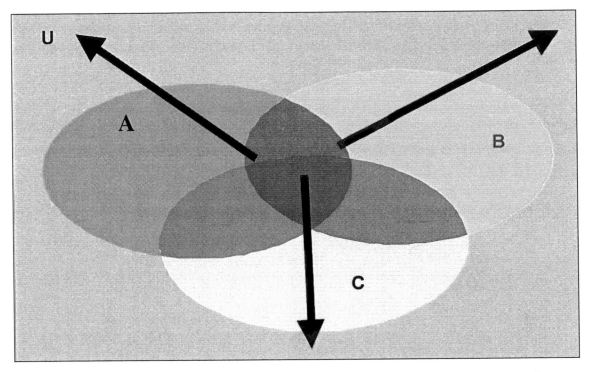

- **U** represents all the different forms of gender-based violence as understood by individuals, groups, communities or countries.

- **A**, **B** and **C** represent individuals, groups, communities or countries. Each of these (individual, group, community or country) would recognise a basic set of 'acts' that are unarguably manifestations of gender-based violence.

- What do we get out of this situation?

  - There will be 'acts' regarded exclusively by **A**, **B** or **C** as acts of gender-based violence.

  - Clearly while there may generally be variation in interpretation of what constitutes gender-based violence across the three groups for example, there will be areas where groups **A and B**, or **A and C**, or **B and C**, or all three, agree that certain acts indeed constitute gender-based violence.

- What is the likely impact?

  - Views exclusively held by **A**, **B** or **C** are likely to be dismissed as unimportant or not sufficiently significant to the common good of all.
  - Views shared by any two groups could be negotiated and probably adopted, but could easily be seen as an imposition by the third group. This could lead to diminished commitment from the third group.
  - All groups will commonly share some views on what constitutes gender-based violence.

- The area of complete agreement on what constitutes gender-based violence by all involved is an important entry point. This consensus allows for the development of effective redress strategies based on a full appreciation of the problem.

- However, the area of total agreement is usually too small to cover all the necessary interventions. Therefore the challenge for all involved is to negotiate for the expansion of the area of total agreement to include other forms of gender-based violence that would be new additions to those previously acknowledged by each group.

- As the base of what constitutes gender-based violence expands, so will scope and capacity for addressing it in different forms.

Session 3: The Legal Framework

The National Legal Framework

This is a technical session that will need legal expertise. It is therefore highly recommended that a lawyer or a person with relevant legal training be identified to facilitate this session. S/he should also be able to supplement the information provided for this session.

During the session the legal expert will take notes and identify the inherent gaps. At the end of the session the legal expert will fill in the gaps by presenting the laws which are relevant to GBV, the structures and mechanisms for accessing justice, the limitations and recommendations to improve these laws, based on group and plenary discussions.

- Some countries have specific gender and/women in development policies that call for the participation of all women and men in the development process.

- Most countries have well-established laws, provisions and procedures, which provide a legal framework through which GBV and human rights are addressed.

- These provisions include criminal laws, civil laws, procedural laws, policies and procedures.

- Although these procedures, laws and policy frameworks exist, they have limitations as indicated below:

  - implementing structures are strongly male-dominated;

  - implementing officers interpret the laws, based on their experiences and discretion, usually influenced by cultural orientation;

  - law enforcement officers have the discretion to suspend or caution the offender;

  - proving the case beyond reasonable doubt is burdensome on the prosecution;

  - as most women are dependent on men, some of them withdraw cases and this is usually encouraged by the charging officers;

  - focussing on punishment as opposed to the needs of the victim, results in repeated victimisation;

  - the courtroom is a stressful environment for the victim;

  - criminal procedures discourage survivors from reporting;

  - law enforcement agents are reluctant to implement judicial decisions;

  - conflicting laws exist which advantage men;

  - the requirements under procedural laws, such as corroboration, make it difficult to get a conviction;

  - provocation as a defence, does not consider the cumulative impact of GBV on women who murder or commit serious crimes against their abusers;

  - the existence of some acts of violence that are grounded in culture;

  - law enforcement officers' lack of training and awareness in gender, human rights and the law;

  - the lack of interventions targeting the perpetrator and the inadequacy of rehabilitation programmes;

- most women and men's unfamiliarity with the national legal framework so they have no choice but to opt for non-formal structures to resolve conflict;

- some insensitive judicial officers, who do not take into account the needs and interests of victims;

- the court process such as recording statements, identification parades, release of perpetrators on bail, exposes survivors to more trauma and discourages them from reporting;

- the existence of a dual system which leaves victims 'forum shopping' for the relevant courts to handle their cases;

- lack of a clear definition of what constitutes GBV;

- the inadequacy or the absence of laws to address specific violations such as sexual harassment.

The International Instruments and Mechanisms

- The international community has developed frameworks and principles on human rights issues that impose obligations on States Parties.

- These instruments provide a framework within which different countries can deal with the problem of GBV.

- Most countries have signed and ratified these international instruments.

- Some have even incorporated these principles into their national constitutions and laws.

- Most of these instruments are highlighted below.

International and Regional Instruments Relevant to GBV

International Conventions that have a direct bearing on gender violence include the following:

The Universal Declaration of Human Rights (UDHR, 1948)

- Article 1 states that all human beings are born free and equal in dignity and human rights.

- Article 2 states that 'everyone is entitled to all the rights and freedoms set forth in the declaration, without distinction of any kind, such as ... sex, or other status'.

- Article 3 states that everyone has the right to life, liberty and security of the person.

- Article 5 states that no one shall be subjected to torture or cruel, inhuman or degrading treatment.

The above provisions indicate that violence against women violates human rights.

The International Covenant on Civil and Political Rights (ICCPR, 1966)

- Article 2 has the same non-discriminatory clause as UDHR.

- Article 6 protects the right to life.

- Article 7 has a similar provision to Article 5 of UDHR.

- Article 9.1 protects the right to liberty and security of the person.

The covenant covers issues of gender-based violence.

The International Covenant on Economic, Social and Cultural Rights (ICESCR, 1966)

- Article 3 guarantees the equal rights of women and men as set out in the covenant, and many of the rights cannot be enjoyed if there is widespread GBV.

- Article 7 guarantees everyone a right to the enjoyment of just and favourable conditions of work. This by implication requires that women should be free from sexual harassment in the workplace and anywhere else.

The Fourth Geneva Convention Protecting Civilians in Times of War (1952)

This convention puts a duty on states to protect women from acts of rape, forced prostitution or any forms of indecent assault, uniting with criminal acts and the Yugoslavia tribunals.

The Convention on the Elimination of all Forms of Discrimination Against Women (CEDAW, 1980)

- Article 1 prohibits discrimination in the social, economic, political and cultural fields.

- General Recommendation 12 requires states to include in their periodic reports, information about violence against women and the measures taken to eliminate such violence.

- General Recommendation 14 calls on states to eliminate female genital mutilation (FGM).

- General Recommendation 19 deals with violence against women and states that GBV is a form of discrimination, which inhibits a woman's ability to enjoy her rights and freedoms on a basis of equality with men, and asks that states party to the convention, to take cognisance of this when reviewing their laws and policies.

CEDAW Optional Protocol (1999)

- This allows individuals and groups, to bring a petition before the CEDAW Committee. NGOs and groups can represent individuals with the consent of such individual victims.

- The committee is given investigative powers on reports of persistent acts of violations of women's rights (but states can opt out of this procedure).

The UN Declaration on the Elimination of Violence against Women (DEVAW, 1993)

- Article 1 defines gender violence as 'any act of gender-based violence that results in, or is likely to result in, physical, sexual, physiological harm or suffering to women, including threats of such acts, coercion or arbitrary deprivation of liberty, whether occurring in private or in public spheres'.

- It recognises that gender violence is rooted historically in unequal power relations.

- It recognises that it occurs in the family, community and is perpetuated by the state and during armed conflict.

It puts a duty on states:

- not to invoke religion or customs to justify violence against women;

- to set standards to prevent prostitution;

- to set standards to prevent, prosecute and punish perpetrators of violence against women, whether it occurs in private or public;

- to change laws, create national plans of action, train members of the criminal justice system, engage in research and collect detailed statistics on issues of violence against women.

The Rome Statute of the International Criminal Court

- This brings gender-related crimes and sexual violence, within the jurisdiction of the international criminal court. The statute affirms that rape, sexual slavery, forced prostitution, forced sterilisation, forced pregnancy and any other form of sexual violence is a crime against humanity.

The Convention on Consent of Marriage; Age of Marriage and Registration of Marriages

- This obliges states that are party to the convention to take measures to abolish customs, laws and practices which impede a woman's choice of a spouse, to eliminate child marriages and to provide penalties .

The United Nations Conventions Against Torture and Other Cruel, Inhuman or Degrading Treatment or Punishment

- These conventions put an obligation on states that are party to the convention, to take legislative, administrative, judicial or other measures to prevent acts of torture within their jurisdiction.

The Conventions on the Rights of the Child (CRC)

- These conventions oblige states that are party to the convention, to take legislative, administrative and other measures to protect children from physical or mental torture, injury, abuse, neglect, negligent treatment, mistreatment, or exploitation, including sexual abuse.

The Declaration on the Protection of Women and Children in Emergency and Armed Conflict

- This states that bombing civilian populations and inflicting suffering on women and other vulnerable groups is forbidden.

Regional Instruments

The Inter-American Convention on the Prevention, Punishment and Eradication of Violence Against Women

- This has provisions similar to CEDAW, but also puts a duty on states to educate people with regard to gender violence.

- It requires states to make periodic reports on what they have done to eliminate gender violence.

- It allows individuals to petition to the Commission set up by the Convention when aggrieved.

The African Charter on Human and People's Rights

- Article 18(3) puts a duty on states to ensure the elimination of discrimination against women and ensure the protection of the rights of women and children as stipulated in international declarations and instruments.

- Although not concise, states are mandated to do all in their power to eliminate any form of discrimination against women, including practices that constitute violence against women.

The OAU has drafted a protocol on the rights of women.

The African Charter on the Rights of the Child:
The charter puts responsibilities on states to observe the following articles:

- Article XVI: which protects children from abuse and torture;

- Article XXI: which protects children against harmful, social and cultural practices;

- Article XXII: which protects children in armed conflict;

- Article XXVII: which protects children from sexual exploitation;

- Article XXIX: which protects children from violent acts or practices including sale, trafficking and abduction.

Declarations and Recommendations from International Conferences

- The 1985 Nairobi forward-looking strategies.

- In 1993, at the UN World Conference on Human Rights in Vienna, countries condemned gender violence and agreed to work towards its elimination in public and private life. The Conference adopted the Vienna Declaration which emphasises the elimination of GBV as follows:

  Article 1 paragraph 18 provides that the human rights of women and the girl child are an inalienable, integral and indivisible part of human rights indicating that:

  - GBV and all forms of sexual harassment and exploitation, including those resulting from cultural prejudice and international trafficking, are incompatible with the dignity and worth of the human being, and must be eliminated;

  - women's human rights should form an integral part of the United Nations human rights activities, including the promotion of all human rights instruments relating to women;

  - governments and other organisations must intensify their efforts for the protection and promotion of all human rights including that of the girl child;

  - the states committed themselves to work towards the elimination of all forms of sexual harassment, exploitation and trafficking in women (part II paragraph 38);

  - gender biases in the administration of justice should be eliminated and any conflicts should be eradicated, which may occasion bias against women, including the harmful effects of certain traditional and customary practices, cultural prejudices and religious extremism;

  - violations of women's rights in conflict situations can be defined as violations of fundamental principles of international humanitarian law, particularly murder, systematic rape, slavery and forced pregnancy.

- On 22 February 1993, the United Nations Security Council, acting under Chapter VII of the United Nations Charter, decided to establish an International Tribunal for the Prosecution of Persons responsible for Serious Violations of International Humanitarian Law Committed in the Territory of the Former Yugoslavia. Unlike the statutes governing the international military tribunals established after the Second World War, the mandate of the current tribunal contains an explicit reference to rape and other sexual offences against women and children.

- In December 1993, the United Nations General Assembly agreed on the Declaration on the Elimination of Violence against Women. In March 1994 the UN Secretary-

General appointed a Special Rapporteur on Violence against Women, its causes and consequences. The Special Rapporteur on Violence against Women receives complaints, investigates and reports on cases of persistent violence against women.

- In 1995 at the UN World Conference on Women in Beijing, GBV was identified as one of the critical areas of concern. In the Beijing Platform for Action Section D identifies strategic measures to be taken by governments to prevent and eliminate violence against women. These include:

  - implementing integrated measures to prevent and eliminate violence against women;

  - studying the causes and consequences of gender violence and the effectiveness of preventive measures;

  - eliminating trafficking in women and assisting victims of violence due to prostitution and trafficking;

Section E of the strategic objectives requires states to:

  - increase the participation of women in conflict resolution at decision-making levels, and protect women living in conflict situations of armed conflicts or under foreign occupation;

  - promote non-violent forms of conflict resolution and reduce the incidence of abuse in conflict and other situations;

SADC Declaration on Gender and Development (1997) and its Addendum: Prevention and the Eradication of Violence Against Women and Children (1998) stipulates that states that are party to the declaration have committed themselves to:

- review land reform laws, amend constitutions and change social practices which still subject women to alienation;

- protect and promote the rights of women and children;

- take urgent action to prevent, and deal with hidden cases of violence against women and children;

- adopt measures in the legal, social, economic, cultural and political fields, educate and create awareness to address violence against women and children in an integrated manner.

Despite the development of these international instruments, the following limitations exist.

- In most countries, signature or ratification does not make the instrument binding because these international standards are not directly applicable. Most countries have to enact national laws to make the instruments binding,

- While many countries have signed and ratified international standards, they have not enacted national laws to effect those standards at national level.

- Some countries have not signed or ratified these instruments.

- Many policymakers, legislators, women, men and law enforcement officers are not aware of the contents of these international laws.

- Some states have signed, but expressed reservations about some articles.

- The international enforcement mechanisms do not bind the country to implement them. They are only bound to report.

- Some countries that have signed, have incorporated the principles of these instrument into their laws, policies and programmes. The challenge now is to implement them.

Mechanisms and Support Systems

- Each country has adopted mechanisms to implement laws relating to gender violence, depending on their legal systems and administrative arrangements.

- In many countries, the following institutions exist for the implementation of the law:

  - **Legal Institutions** – women's departments, judicial institutions, educational institutions, research organisations, structures on gender violence and education, community level structures and other departments;

  - **Police** – personnel who are responsible for arresting, investigating and prosecuting cases;

  - **Department of Public Affairs Prosecutions (DPP)** – a department run by professional staff whose role is to prosecute cases;

  - **Ministry of Legal Affairs/Justice** – a department responsible for the overall administration of the law;

  - **Social Welfare/Probation** – which handles complaints relating to family matters and provides counselling and other related services;

  - **Judiciary** – which involves courts at all levels for the adjudication of cases;

  - **Health Department** – staffed with personnel to treat victims and perpetrators;

  - **NGOs** – organisations involved in legal aid, legal education, research, advocacy counselling and the provision of other services,

  - **Commissions** – such as human rights, equal opportunities, law reform and the ombudsman. These institutions have as one of their mandates to investigate and settle some of the cases.

  - **Department of Prisons** – a department which provides custody for those who have been convicted.

Interventions

By Relevant Bodies

Government, departments, Non-Governmental Organisations (NGOs) and Community Based Organisations (CBOs) have devised different strategies as interventions for combating GBV.

The interventions include reform of the legal system, provision of services to both victim and perpetrator, capacity building, public education and awareness campaigns.

By the Criminal Justice System

The interventions are designed to punish the perpetrator and stop further occurrences of violence. These include the following:

confinement (depending on the severity of the offence); supervision; binding orders; compensation; caution and advisory services.

These orders are discretionary and the magistrate or the judge can choose from the different options.

Services to victims which include:

- hotlines, shelter/drop-in centres support units, homes, evacuation procedures, medical care, counselling for the victim, legal aid and support of victims during the trial;

- counselling, supervision, rehabilitation and psychiatric treatment for the perpetrators.

Public Education

Legal education is designed to influence values, attitudes and behaviour. It includes the following:

- workshops/seminars; the production of leaflets/booklets to disseminate information on relevant topics; radio/television programmes; drama; songs; and violence against women campaigns.

The Limitations

- Most interventions try to address the immediate needs of the victim (i.e. providing shelter).

- Other interventions are designed to address the future needs of the victim, such as counselling, so that they can cope or live with the acts of violence.

- Some are designed to rehabilitate, change and prevent future occurrences of acts of violence.

- Other interventions are designed to change the attitudes and behaviour of society.

  However, such interventions have the following limitations:

- The criminal justice system only punishes to prevent future occurrences, but does not address the cause of the offence.

- Most interventions address one cause and not other related factors such as unequal power relations in society.

- The law is not applied systematically for example, when a case is reported, a survivor may withdraw the case, because she is dependent on the perpetrator or she fears reprisals from the family. Yet in most countries, there is no mandatory prosecution, especially in cases where there is enough evidence to prosecute and when the victim is willing to press charges.

- The system does not cater for the needs of the victim, for example her moral character may be brought into question.

- The victim often suffers trauma as a result of "a courtroom which is intimidating" and may be discouraged from continuing with the case.

- The survivor often has to return to the same environment as the perpetrator.

- Medical officers are not trained to identify cases of GBV; as a result many cases are not reported.

- Counselling is a private matter and does not send a signal to society that GBV is a serious crime. It may focus on the victim who may end up thinking she is to blame.

- In the African context, few people seek psychological treatment and therefore counselling the perpetrator may not help.

- Programmes designed to change cultural attitudes, may be viewed as an attack on cultural values and may cause a backlash for women.

You will need to identify the victims, that is, those who are affected by GBV, those who want to abolish it, and those who perpetuate it.

Identify men, cultural leaders, who would be interested in seeing that it ends, and those who would assist such as NGOs, CBOs, activists, employers, institutions and politicians.

Problems of Enforcement

- Most interventions focus on punishing or rehabilitating the offender and do not prevent repeated behaviour.

- There is limited support available for the relevant agencies where they exist.

- Staff may not be trained to handle essential equipment.

- Most institutions are male-dominated and therefore are not sensitive to women's needs and interests.

- There is a lack of specific policies and national plans to address GBV.

- There is limited capacity in terms of geographical coverage, equipment, transport and other resources.

- Most people in those institutions have limited training on gender issues.

- Resources (human and financial) are limited, so most services are confined to urban areas.

- There are few women in decision-making positions who can effectively influence policies and programmes to address GBV.

- Most service providers have limited networks and often do not co-ordinate effectively, so there are limited interventions and increasing duplication, which results in the inefficient use of resources.

- There are inadequate linkages among the various individuals within the criminal justice system.

- Most national machineries for women have no legal departments, nor do they employ legal professionals to advise on issues relevant to GBV.

Social Problems

- Women have been socialised to accept their inferior position.

- Low levels of education among the women means they cannot get well-paid jobs to sustain themselves and are therefore dependent on men. However, recent debates have shown that even economically independent women suffer from abuse.

- There is a perception that women are physically weak.

- Stress results in violent behaviour and violent upbringing leads to violence. Hence a child who has grown up in an abusive situation can also be violent.

- Poor self control on the part of men.

- Because of different opportunities, men and women have different access to resources, which means different levels of power, an imbalance which renders women powerless.

Legal Problems
- discriminatory laws for example, women cannot inherit land in many societies;

- arbitrary procedural rules;

- inadequate enforcement mechanisms;

- lack of enforcement of recommendations arising from GBV studies.

How to Improve the Efficiency of Current Mechanisms
There is a need for:

- effective co-ordination in order to expand networks;

- more facilities, including human and financial resources;

- the development of training programmes especially on gender issues;

- the enactment of relevant laws to provide a comprehensive legal framework;

- development of the profile of the victims and perpetrators in order to understand the physical and psychological character of a victim of violence and an assessment of how these translate into needs. This should also include understanding the perpetrator.

Session 4: Sharing Experiences and Challenges

To facilitate this session, participating organisations should be asked to prepare a brief summary covering the overall objectives, activities, achievements, challenges, and partners – including potential ones.

- Stakeholders dealing with issues of GBV are critical for its eradication. These stakeholders have gained substantial experience in the area of GBV and organisations continue to share these experiences and lessons.

- Programmes and activities have been undertaken by organisations emphasising self-esteem, associative strengths and resourcefulness and in some cases joint action planning. However a number of challenges exist for organisations dealing with GBV.

The Challenges

- lack of financial/human resources including a limited capacity in fundraising initiatives and techniques;

- inadequate government support and limited political will and commitment from decision-makers who control resources;

- fear of loss of identity often expressed by organisations, which undermines the efforts of collective action planning and responsibility;

- lack of sharing financial and human resources, which could render their efforts effective and could avoid duplication;

- lack of diverse skills, capacity and expertise among GBV stakeholders. Essential skills include networking, financial sustainability, effective management practice, service delivery and good governance.

For these stakeholders to meet the challenges stated above there is a need for them to:

- involve relevant government departments, the private sector and NGOs;

- realise that GBV is a social problem as well as a public and development issue that calls for a multidisciplinary response involving state and non-state participants;

- understand that although they have different perceptions and attitudes, they are all working towards one critical goal of eradicating GBV;

- recognise that establishing solid partnerships will increase their bargaining power with decision-makers who control economic resources;

- appreciate the fact that establishing functional mechanisms for networking, co-ordination and collaboration, will earn them tangible, verifiable results in GBV interventions;

- understand that sharing resources will result in using the resources optimally and reduce duplication;

- understand that working in isolation will not yield results;

- recognise that reaching the consumers of the GBV interventions in a fragmented manner will only confuse them.

Stakeholders therefore need to establish a common identity for the achievement of a common goal. Establishing a stakeholder enrolment and involvement process should facilitate working towards this common goal. Stakeholders include government departments and institutions, NGOs, the private sector, media and development agencies.

Session 5: The Frameworks for Addressing GBV

What is the Gender Management System (GMS)?

- A Gender Management System is a Commonwealth approach to gender mainstreaming.

- It is a network of structures, mechanisms and processes.

- These are put in place within an existing organisational framework.

- The purpose is to guide, plan, monitor and evaluate the process of mainstreaming gender, into all areas of the organisation's work, in order to achieve greater equality and equity within the context of sustainable development.

- It can be established at any level of government or in institutions such as universities, intergovernmental organisations, NGOs and the private sector.

What is the GMS Mission?

The mission of a GMS is to advance gender equality and equity through:

- promoting political will;

- forging a partnership of stakeholders including government, the private sector and civil society;

- building capacity;

- sharing good practice.

What is its Goal?

The GMS goal is to mainstream gender into all government policies, programmes and activities.

The **GMS objectives** are to:

- assist governments and non-state participants in implementing the 1995 Commonwealth Plan of Action on Gender and Development and its Update (2000-2005);

- strengthen national women's machineries to direct and co-ordinate national gender mainstreaming efforts;

- strengthen the capacity of government ministries and non-state participants, to ensure that gender is systematically and consistently mainstreamed into their policies, plans and programmes;

- create an enabling environment.

The GMS Stakeholder Approach to Gender Mainstreaming

The GMS adopts a stakeholder approach based on three broad principles, which are:

empowerment, integration and accountability.

The essential elements of a GMS are an enabling environment, which calls for:

- the political will of governments;
- the allocation of adequate human and financial resources;
- the formulation of legislative and administrative frameworks;
- placing women in decision-making positions at all levels;
- the active involvement of civil society.

The **GMS process** involves:

- setting up GMS structures and instituting support mechanisms;
- developing and implementing a national gender action plan;
- mainstreaming gender into the national development plan, as well as plans and programmes of sectoral ministries.

GMS structures consist of the following:

- the lead agency;
- gender focal points/inter-ministerial steering committee;
- a Parliamentary gender caucus;
- gender equality Commission/Council.

GMS mechanisms take into consideration:

- undertaking gender analysis programmes;
- providing gender training;
- installing management information systems;
- instituting performance appraisal systems.

The GMS in Action

GMS has been introduced to 13 Commonwealth countries. It has been successfully applied to government budgets and violence against women.

Application of Gender Management (GMS) Principles to Combating Gender-based Violence

Gender Management Systems (GMS)

At a glance!

Background

How did GMS come into being?

- Efforts by countries to promote equality of opportunities and outcomes between women and men
- Generations of conceptualisation and corresponding programme development
- 5WAMM – Some progress made in addressing gender gaps, gender mainstreaming efforts intermittent, lack of coordination, difficulties in determining national aggregate performance
- Mandate

Examples of application questions: Do women and men experience GBV the same way? How is the achievement of gender equity likely to affect gender-based violence (GBV)? Is there evidence of unco-ordinated efforts to combat GBV? Is there a clear mandate and commitment for addressing GBV?

What is a GMS?

- A Commonwealth approach for gender mainstreaming
- A network of structures, mechanisms and processes developed within an existing framework
- It should guide and aid the planning, monitoring and evaluation process of integrating gender into all areas of work
- It should lead to enhanced levels of gender equality and equity within the context of sustainable development

Examples of application questions: Is there a need to establish structures, mechanisms and processes in order to eliminate GBV? What is the value added for planning, monitoring and evaluating programmes for combating GBV?

Who can use it?

It can be established at any level of government or institution, intergovernmental organisations, NGOs, CBOs, private sector, etc.

Example of application questions: Which of the listed categories of use would not be appropriate for efforts to combat GBV?

GMS objectives

- To assist state and non-state actors in the implementation of the Commonwealth POA and its Update
- To strengthen the capacity of NWMs to direct, advise and coordinate national gender mainstreaming efforts
- To promote systemic, systematic and consistent gender mainstreaming into policies, plans, programmes and activities
- To create an enabling gender inclusive environment

Examples of application questions: Does the Commonwealth POA and its Update target the elimination of GBV? Is combating GBV a national priority? Does the NWM have capacity for policy advice, advocacy and programme coordination? Is gender sufficiently integrated into current GBV programmes?

GMS stakeholder approach

Broad principles:

Integration

Empowerment

Accountability

Examples of application questions: Who are GBV stakeholders? How can we strengthen stakeholder integration, empowerment and accountability for more holistic GBV programme initiatives?

GMS essential components

- Enabling environment
- The GMS process
- GMS structures
- GMS mechanisms

Example(s) of application questions: How can an enabling environment be created and a clear process, functional structures as well as facilitative mechanisms be established, for eliminating GBV?

GMS mission

To advance gender equality and equity through

- Promoting political will
- Forging a partnership of stakeholders
- Building capacity
- Sharing good practice

Examples of application questions: Is political will essential for combating GBV? Is there a need to develop stakeholder partnerships in efforts to eliminate GBV? Is there a need to build capacity to address GBV? Is there a need for enhanced sharing of good practice?

The Integrated Approach

Attempts have been made by the following institutions to address GBV at national, regional and international levels.

- In 1990, the United Nations Expert Group called for an integrated approach, where there is a partnership between the criminal justice system, service providers and those involved in creating awareness.

- The First Conference of European Ministries of Physical and Sexual Violence called for an integrated approach dealing with law, procedural aspects, assistance and relief for victims, perpetrators and carrying out general research.

- The Beijing Platform for Action called for integrated measures to prevent and eliminate violence against women.

- The Commonwealth Women's Affairs Ministers at their meetings in 1996 and 2000 also recommended the use of an integrated approach to address violence against women. The Commonwealth Secretariat designed the framework after noting that gender violence is a multifaceted problem and has to be addressed in a co-ordinated manner.

- The SADC Declaration on Gender and Development and its Addendum, called for an integrated approach to GBV.

Government, NGOs, CBOs and individuals have also developed strategies to address GBV, but the problem persists due to factors including:

- different individuals/groups work in isolation and lack co-ordination;

- most countries lack national policy frameworks and plans of action to address GBV;

- lack of systematic ways of keeping data to enable governments or NGOs to develop relevant interventions.

Why the Integrated Approach

- It is designed to assist governments, the private sector, civil society and other agencies to understand GBV as a multi-faceted problem that should be addressed in a holistic manner.

- The framework enables government to review its position regarding GBV, conceptualise it as a social problem as well as a public and development issue, provide a policy framework and plan of action, and allocate resources to address it.

There are many organisations trying to address the problem. We need to build on current efforts. There is a need to address the matter by both the private and public stakeholders in a co-ordinated manner to achieve results.

The Advantages of an Integrated Approach

The integrated approach has the following advantages:

- improved co-ordination and collaboration among different stakeholders which enhances efficiency in the delivering of services, in support of victims, survivors, perpetrators of GBV and other affected persons;

- enables governments to address violence against women as a complex social problem that requires an overall national policy framework and a plan of action;

- encourages service providers to form comprehensive units and wider networks through which services can be delivered;

- encourages allocation and optimal use of resources, and the experience and expertise of the different individuals/groups and stakeholders are brought together;

- increases the information base, making service delivery more efficient;

- improves advocacy campaigns as more participants are involved;

- strengthens preventive strategies which are often ignored;

- encourages systematic recording statistics and the sharing of information.

The Step-by-Step Approach

Why the integrated approach?

It will assist state and non-state participants to eliminate GBV through:

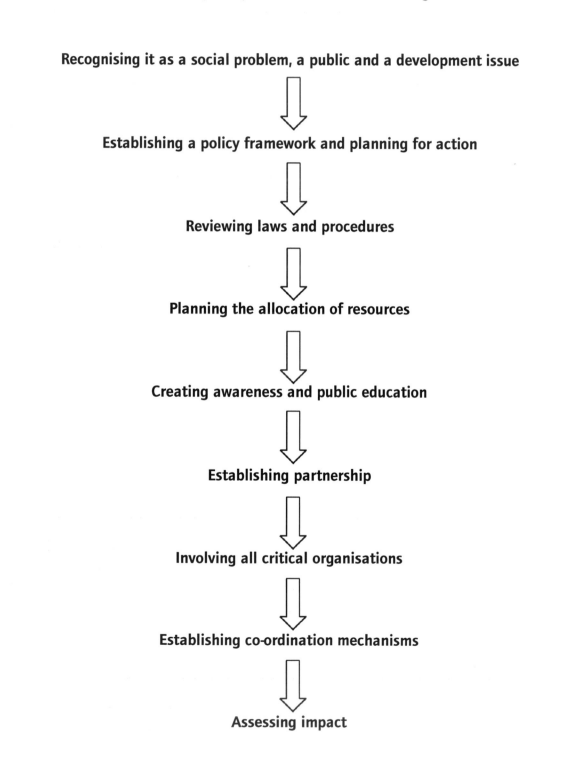

Recognising it as a social problem, a public and a development issue

Establishing a policy framework and planning for action

Reviewing laws and procedures

Planning the allocation of resources

Creating awareness and public education

Establishing partnership

Involving all critical organisations

Establishing co-ordination mechanisms

Assessing impact

Advantages of an Integrated Approach

An integrated approach has the following advantages:

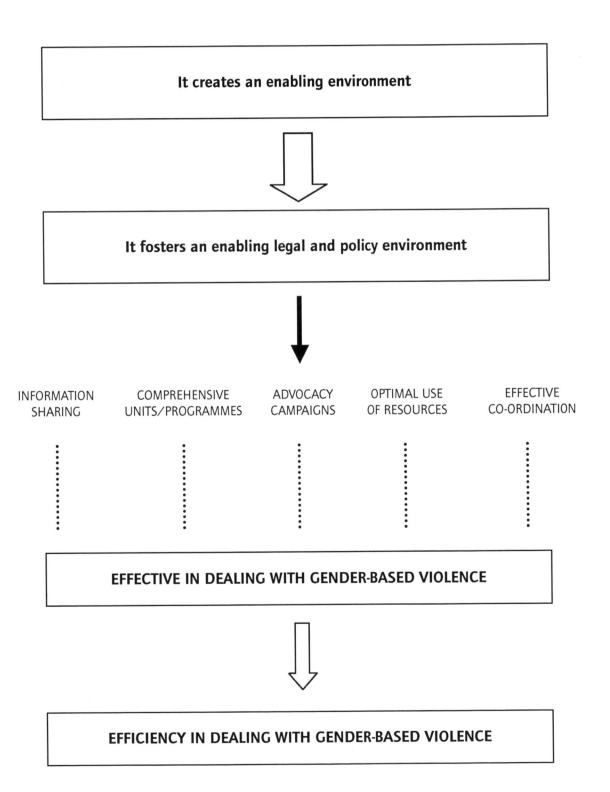

It creates an enabling environment

It fosters an enabling legal and policy environment

| INFORMATION SHARING | COMPREHENSIVE UNITS/PROGRAMMES | ADVOCACY CAMPAIGNS | OPTIMAL USE OF RESOURCES | EFFECTIVE CO-ORDINATION |

EFFECTIVE IN DEALING WITH GENDER-BASED VIOLENCE

EFFICIENCY IN DEALING WITH GENDER-BASED VIOLENCE

ASSUMPTIONS OF THE MODEL

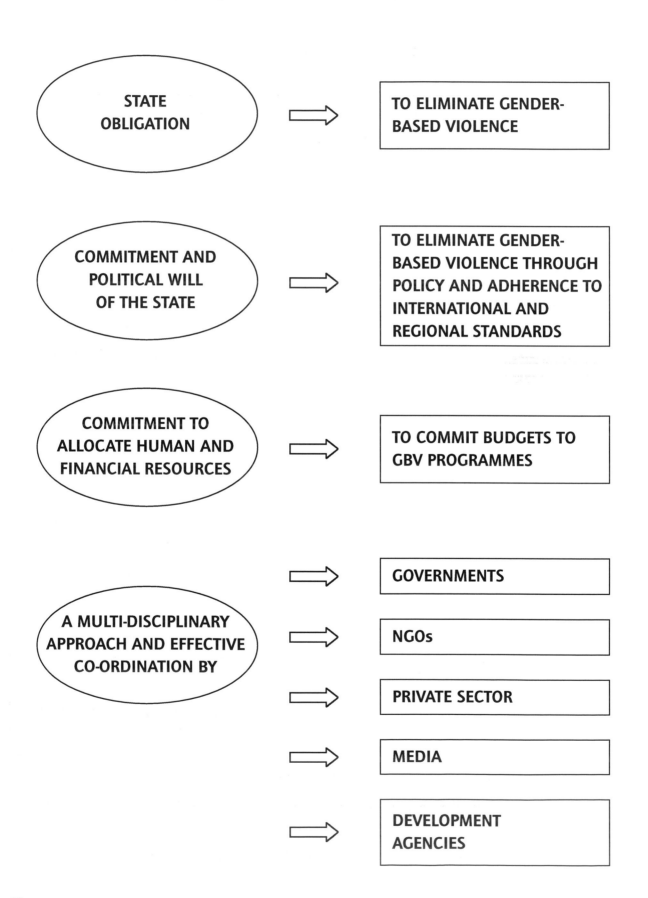

The Key Elements of an Integrated Approach
The following steps indicate key components of the integrated approach. Additional points are presented below each step and may be used to elaborate.

Step 1
Conceptualisation of the Problem

- Understand the problem to determine the response and seek solutions.
- View GBV as a social and not a private matter.
- Establish a framework to deal with GBV.
- Establish co-ordination mechanisms.
- Do not view GBV from a narrow perspective, it is a complex issue and its nature, causes, extent and consequences are difficult and deep-rooted.

- Most governments do not view GBV as a social problem, but as a private matter that does not require government intervention.
- The way we view a problem will determine our responses. If a matter is seen as a problem, then we begin to seek solutions.
- When action is taken, it is done randomly without a framework.
- There is no purposeful co-ordination between the critical participants.
- Interventions are viewed narrowly by different bodies.

It should be seen as a complex problem, which is complex in nature.

Step 2
A Deeper Understanding of the Problem

- Following conceptualisation of the problem, seek to understand the symptoms as well as the root causes of GBV.
- Understand GBV from the point of view of the victim, perpetrator, family and other affected individuals, the community and the state.

Understand that GBV is not a private matter.

Enrol all stakeholders, that is, those who work directly or indirectly to combat GBV, perpetrators, victims and survivors of GBV, and those who want to maintain the status quo.

This second step is closely linked to the first.

- Once the problem has been conceptualised we realise that our understanding of the problem is limited.
- This has often led to people addressing the symptoms and not the causes.

- It is important to understand the causes and consequences where they relate to the victim, perpetrators, the family, community and the state.

- This understanding is critical, otherwise the matter will continue to be treated as private.

- The stakeholders should be defined, that is those interested in eliminating the problem and who can help to develop strategies to implement actions.

Involve different stakeholders within government, the private sector and among NGOs.

Understanding Causes, Consequences and Stakeholder Contribution
By:

- carrying out surveys and research;

- establishing networks;

- listening to different parties;

- confronting the perpetrators;

- visiting complainants regularly;

- training trainers and paralegals;

- training traditional counsellors and religious leaders;

- developing gender sensitisation and analysis programmes;

- developing instruments for data collection;

- collecting data;

- compiling and analysing data, writing reports and disseminating information.

Responding to the Needs of the Victim
In responding to the needs of the victim there is a need to:

- provide temporary refuge for women and minor children;

- provide legal advice and counselling;

- empower women economically;

- assist victims to apply for protection orders;

- assist victims to report matters to the police;

- visit victims in their homes;

- accompany victims to hospitals and shelters;

- provide social support to victims;

- identify areas where centres can be established;

- improve facilities in existing centres;

- develop guidelines for training;

- train personnel to handle cases;

- acquire the necessary equipment;
- create awareness among communities and produce training materials.

Responding to the Perpetuator

By:

- counselling and follow up;
- issuing protection orders;
- referrals to specialised services;
- conducting inquiries;
- developing posters, pamphlets; drama workshops; mobile clinics;
- running in-service training courses in prisons, including lobbying and advocacy.

Step 3

Develop Actions and Strategies

- Develop a policy framework and an implementation strategy.
- Set long- and short-term objectives.
- Determine the actions and strategies to be taken.
- Identify the relevant bodies.
- Set indicators for monitoring action.
- Identify sources of funding.
- Set a timeframe to achieve the targets.
- State assumptions and constraints.

- Once the problem, causes and consequences have been understood, then action is taken in a more meaningful manner. The action should be designed to address the root causes, consequences and the strategies towards its elimination. The action strategies will involve:
  - developing a policy framework;
  - setting short- and long-term objectives;
  - determining the actions to be taken;
  - identifying the relevant bodies, including the support agencies;
  - setting indicators for monitoring progress in action;
  - identifying sources of funding;
  - setting time limits for the achievement of targets.

The overall goal of the action strategies should be to eliminate GBV.

Step 4

Co-ordination

- Involve all stakeholders dealing with GBV and share information regularly.

- Avoid duplication of efforts among stakeholders.

- Utilise resources in the best possible way.

- Institutionalise components of the plan of action, according to the critical areas of intervention of the various key stakeholders.

Step 5

Establish a Co-ordinating Mechanism

Establish a co-ordinating body with a mandate to:

- develop overall policy to be adopted by government;

- co-ordinate policy implementation;

- monitor progress and assess the impact of strategies;

- ensure regular policy reviews;

- respond to new circumstances;

- direct and co-ordinate interventions between different stakeholders.

The different components of the model give rise to the need for co-ordination among the various participants. Linkages are necessary because:

- all stakeholders are dealing with the same problem;

- the different organisations remain informed of what the others are doing and can build on each other's work;

- duplication of efforts can be avoided;

A focal point officer can link these groups to the co-ordinating body.

The co-ordinating body can have the following mandate:

- develop the overall policy to be adopted by government;

- be in charge of implementing policy and overall co-ordination;

- monitor progress and assess the impact of strategies;

- ensure regular policy review;

- respond to new circumstances;

- direct and co-ordinate interventions, while ensuring that the efforts of NGOs are co-ordinated and the efforts of government and other collaborators are monitored.

Linkages must be institutionalised. Build a culture of co-ordination instead of relying on personal/sectoral and fragmented arrangements.

Departments, NGOs and CBOs with similar roles can be grouped together into four units with an immediate objective.

For example, those trying to address the needs of the survivor, those dealing with the perpetrator, those trying to change values, norms and attitudes and those seeking to have a clearer understanding of the problem.

Modify Structures

By:

- enacting laws where they do not exist, such as those pertaining to sexual harassment;
- reforming discriminatory laws;
- organising advocacy education and awareness campaigns;
- educating women, men and policymakers on the law;
- modifying procedures;
- collecting information;
- modifying laws to incorporate international standards;
- providing gender training for people who are in different structures;
- providing resources;
- providing facilities.

Build the Capacity of Government, NGOs, Private Sector and CBOs

By:

- developing a policy framework;
- co-ordinating the efforts of stakeholders;
- organising a co-ordinating GBV forum;
- disseminating relevant information through newsletters etc.;
- collecting and compiling data;
- providing training;
- spearheading advocacy campaigns;
- developing a curriculum;
- developing participatory, training and capacity building programmes;
- establishing appropriate institutions, structures and mechanisms.

Change Attitudes and Values

By:

- undertaking needs assessments;
- identifying target groups;
- organising IEC campaigns seminars, talks, media, posters and cartoons;
- producing materials;
- organising seminars, workshops, drama, debates, press conferences, discussion groups, local community radio;
- training trainers and paralegals.

Session 6: Development of the Plan of Action

The facilitator should present and explain the following logical steps for developing a plan of action.

Step 1

Formulating the overall strategy

What is a strategy?

It is an expression of the plan, or broad aim which leads to the achievement of a process.

Example:

To develop a deeper understanding of the extent, nature, causes, consequences and concept of gender-based violence.

Step 2

Formulating the objective, which should be linked to the overall strategy.

What is an objective?

It is an answer to the following questions:

Why are we formulating the strategy?

Why should we have the process, or why is it necessary?

Example:

To create awareness among 50 per cent of community leaders and elders about the extent, nature, causes, consequences and concept of gender-based violence by July 2002.

An objective should be:

- specific to the challenge;
- measurable in terms of quality and quantity;
- achievable to a reasonable extent in relation to the available resources;
- realistic in terms of achievement;
- time bound which means implementable within a stated realistic timeframe.

This is the smart principle generally used in the development of objectives.

Step 3

Development of activities

What are activities?

Activities are actions that should be undertaken to achieve the overall strategy and objective(s).

Examples:

National stakeholders' workshops; focus group discussions at community level; key informant interviews/consultations with community leaders; mini-workshops with women and young persons.

Step 4

Identifying the target group

Who constitutes the target group?

- The target group should consist of stakeholders best placed to address identified needs.
- Therefore, different needs will determine the constitution of appropriate target groups. They could be:
  - those that will benefit from the programme of activities;
  - those that will contribute ideas to GBV interventions;
  - those that can effect change or influence policymakers;
  - those that can give financial, technical and other forms of support.

Examples:

Policymakers, government departments, NGOs, community leaders, politicians, development partners, community-based organisations, other relevant institutions, religious organisations and traditional healers, police commissioners, prosecutors, national curriculum developers.

Step 5

Agreeing on the lead agency.

What is a lead agency? It is a body:

- with leadership, management, co-ordination and negotiation responsibility;
- that has been given a mandate to carry out specific tasks by the government of the country;
- which is recognised by the governments of the country.

Examples:

A council, a gender/women organisation appointed or established by government.

Step 6

Identifying the implementers of the programme.

Who are the implementers?

- They are those stakeholders who should implement, deliver services effectively, have the knowledge and skills, and report adequately on programme delivery.

Examples:

NGOs, government departments, community-based organisations, young people's organisations, extension workers and other social groups.

Step 7
Mobilising resources

What are resources?

- Resources will support the implementation of the programme; these should be human and physical.

Examples:

Funds, expertise, experience, technical advisors, equipment, training and resource materials.

Step 8
Identifying funding agencies.

What are funding agencies?

- Those agencies that can provide financial and other support for programme implementation.

Examples:

Donors, government, NGOs, private sector, individuals.

Step 9
Indicating the timeframe

What is a timeframe?

- The reasonable time for implementing a particular activity.

Examples:

Days, weeks, months and years.

Step 10
Stating indicators.

What are indicators?

- The criteria for success which enables you to measure or assess the achievements of the objectives. Indicators can be qualitative or quantitative.

Examples:

Quantitative indicators
- **Two focus group discussions held with twenty community leaders.**
- **Four workshops held on the international and legal framework, and reports produced and circulated.**

- **Three researchers trained, a study carried out in one region, and a report produced on the extent, nature, causes and consequences of GBV.**

- **Ten percent decrease in reported rape cases in urban areas by 2004.**

Qualitative indicators
- **change in attitudes and behaviour towards issues of GBV among community leaders**

Step 11
Risks and assumptions

What are risks?

- Factors which can prevent the successful implementation of activities.

Examples:

Lack of adequate financial and human resources, lack of information and empirical data, lack of stakeholder enrolment and involvement.

What are assumptions?

- Factors that can contribute to the successful implementation of the activities.

Example:

Political will by governments to address GBV, all stakeholders agreeing to co-operate. Funds made available by governments.

Intersperse the presentation with questions to check understanding.

Restate information to increase understanding.

Use the information generated by participants during the group discussions to record key issues.

Evaluating the Workshop

- Evaluating the training is a valuable part of learning.

- It can be the liveliest part of the training event.

- Participants should be given an opportunity to evaluate the training.

- This is an opportunity for them to express their feelings freely about the activities, sessions or the whole workshop programme.

Evaluation can be approached from the following angles:

You can evaluate as the workshop proceeds, i.e. drawing out the learning points from each activity session. For example: What three important points have you learnt in the activity or session? How could we have done better?

- You can design a written evaluation form with the following questions:

  - Were the objectives of the workshop met?

  - In your opinion which objectives were not sufficiently met?

  - What did you like about the workshop?

  - What key issues will you take back with you to improve your organisations, that will help to address GBV?

  - What can be improved if a similar workshop is organised?

- You can do a participatory evaluation by asking each participant the following questions:

  - What key issues can you draw from the sessions?

  - What can be improved in the future?

You can design questions around the objectives and the outputs and divide participants in groups to respond to the questions stated below;

  - Did we meet every objective that we set forth to meet? Give reasons.

  - What were the outputs of each session?

  - Did we reach a consensus on the output?

  - How can we do better next time?

Ice-Breakers, Openers/Methods for the Introductory Session

The Name Game
- What is it?

It is a game or an opener related to the subject matter.

- Why is it used?

It is used to make participants relax, to remove any reservations that they bring with them to the workshop, to allow them to get to know each other and to become one community.

- When is it used?

It is used at the beginning of the workshop during the introductory activity.

- How is it used?

Tell participants that we will give ourselves new names for the workshop. The new names should rhyme with the first letter of their real names. Encourage participants to relate the new names to the workshop theme. Start by giving yourself a new name to set an example, and to make them feel that you are one among equals.

Examples:

Persuasive Patricia	Violent Veronica	Enabling Elizabeth
Legalistic Lillian	Batterer Ben	Participatory Peter

The names should be used throughout the workshop.

The 'But Why?' Method
- What is it?

It is a participatory approach to training.

- Why is it used?

It is used to achieve a deeper understanding of an issue or a problem, to persuade participants to have fun, and as an energiser.

- When is it used?

It can be used at the beginning of the training or during the sessions/activities.

- How is it used?

Distribute the following example to different groups:

Peter battered Elizabeth very badly. *But why?*

Because Elizabeth talked back. *But why?*

Because women are not allowed to talk back. *But why?*

Because they are subordinate to men. *But why?*

Because it is the culture. *But why?*

Because culture favours men. *But why?*

Because men are heads of households. *But why?*

Because the Bible says so.
Give other examples and do the exercise in groups.

Other examples:

Francis raped his step-daughter. *But why?*

Mavis refused to report to the police that her daughter was raped by her biological father. *But why?*

The judge delivered a minimum sentence of three months in jail for the case of a man who set his wife alight, she sustained third degree burns. *But why?*

Felicity reported to her in-laws that her husband slaps her most of the time, her in-laws took no notice. *But why?*

Jemima was almost beaten to death by the father of her three children, she reported the case and withdrew it after three days. *But why?*

Selinah caught her husband twice with two different women, she suggested to him that they should start using condoms, he refused and threatened to beat her. *But why?*

The Mind-Mapping Technique
- What is it?

It is another type of brainstorming exercise.

- Why is it used?

It is used to generate ideas from the participants about a particular issue to enable them to put these ideas into context.

- When is it used?

It can be used during training sessions to tease out many ideas geared to the formulation of concepts or definitions.

- How is it used?

Draw a big circle or illustration on a flipchart, insert the topic or issue that you are addressing in the middle of the illustration or circle. Ask the following question:

What words are associated with the topic in the middle of the circle?
- Write in the words alongside the circle, using arrows;
- Ask participants in groups to formulate a concept or a definition from the association of words;
- Facilitate a report-back session and agree on concepts and definitions.

The Treasure Hunt
- What is it?

It is one of the participatory methods.

- Why is it used?

It is used to stimulate the participants' thinking process and analytical ability. It can also be used as an icebreaker.

- When is it used?

It can be used at the beginning of the workshop or in between the training sessions.

- How is it used?

Stick information prepared in advance on cards. Place the cards behind or under a chair or table, and even around the training room at strategic points, but the cards must always be hidden. Ask participants to look around for the treasure.

Ask those who have found treasure to stand up, and those who have not to sit down. Each participant then reads out the information on the paper and explains what it means in her/his own words.

The rest of the group is allowed to comment, correct or explain further.

The Mixed Bag Technique

- What is it?

It is one of the participatory methods.

- Why is it used?

It is used to increase the participants' level of involvement.

- When is it used?

It can be used at the beginning, during training, or at the end of the workshop.

- How is it used?

Cut out pieces of paper with different pieces of information on them, which need to be clarified or defined. Put the pieces of paper in a basket, hat or any container. The number of cut-out pieces should be equivalent to the number of participants.

Ask the participants, one by one, to choose a piece of paper from the container. Ask each participant to read out what s/he has picked and explain the information to the rest. Other participants can comment, explain further.

The Secret Ballot Technique

- What is it?

It is one of the participatory methods.

- Why is it used?

It is used to remove inhibitions from participants, especially on topics that are sensitive.

- When is it used?

It is used when dealing with sensitive issues that may raise conflict between target groups.

- How is it used?

Cut out pieces of paper with sensitive topics written on them. Ask each participant, or select a few to pick out one piece of paper from a container. Participants respond to the issue on the paper secretly and drop it back in the container without writing their names on it.

The responses are then shared with the rest of the group and topics are openly discussed and agreed upon.

Some examples of sensitive topics are:

Women are perpetrators as well.

Men do not like sharing responsibilities with women.

Men do not believe that women can lead.

Men can also cook.

Women do not support each other, that is why they cannot be leaders.

Pioneers of the women's movement hate to be displaced by emerging young activists.

Women are the weaker sex.

Women are the ones who provoke men and cause the beatings. They talk too much.

Case Studies, Critical Incidents and Key Informant Views

Critical Incidents for Session 2 Activity 3
Critical Incident 1

At a workshop on the integrated approach to GBV, some men and women put forward this view:

We know that men are in the majority of perpetrators, but because we do not know the extent and nature of GBV, how can we conclude that women too are not perpetrators?

Discussion Questions

- Why did women and men say this?
- Do you agree with the statement? Whether you agree or do not agree, support your argument.

Critical Incident 2

One male participant at one of the workshops on the integrated approach to GBV made the following statement:

Why should all men be labelled perpetrators? Do we not have any decent men? Any man who violates a woman is acting like an animal. Why do we continue to "animalise" men? Why don't we try to remove the animal in him?

Discussion Points

- Analyse this participant's statement.
- Do you agree with it?
- How can we meet this challenge?

Case Study 1: Wife Beating

Judy was married to Sam according to the Iteso custom. She sold tomatoes in the local market to supplement the family income. Her husband's salary could not sustain their family of nine children and five dependent relatives.

One day she returned late at 8.00 p.m., market women had had a meeting. Her husband was already at home and the children were crying for supper. He beat her until she fainted. She was taken to hospital with a broken arm. In hospital she told the doctor that she sustained the fracture when she fell into a ditch. However, her friend Jane insisted that she should take the matter to the police.

Sam was arrested and confessed to beating her. He defended himself by saying that a woman like Judy, who came home late and neglected her children only deserved such a punishment. Because Jane's sister was a lawyer, they advised Judy to press charges. The prosecutor reluctantly went on with the case. During the trial, Judy refused to talk, because all her in-laws were in court and she was afraid to say anything that would blame her husband. As a result, the case was withdrawn. When they went back home, her husband and family met and she was told to leave the home with her children.

- What would have been Judy's chances of getting a conviction in this case?

- What factors do you think made Judy reluctant to pursue the case?

- Even if Judy had proceeded with the case, what legal and procedural rules and other factors would have affected its outcome?

Case Study 2: Defilement

Rose, a nine-year-old girl, came home from school one day and found that her mother was out. But she had left the keys of the house with John, their neighbour. John invited her to his house and forced her to have sex with him.

When her mother returned, she found Rose crying, but she did not tell her mother about it, because she was afraid. A week later, she started to feel a burning pain every time she urinated. Eventually pus started to come out of her genitals, and because of the pain, she was forced to tell her mother, who in turn reported the matter to the police.

When John was arrested, he stated that the girl was lying and that she probably had had sex with a schoolmate. After the police had beaten him, he confessed to having forced the girl to have sex with him. He was later charged with defilement, but during the trial he pleaded not guilty and stated that he was forced by the police to confess.

- What are the chances of getting a conviction in this case?

- What are the legal and procedural factors, which may limit the chances of getting a conviction?

- What other factors limit women's ability to achieve justice in the criminal justice system?

Case Study 3: Murder

Lucy was married to John for three years. Right from the very first day of their marriage, he beat her for any small mistake. For example when she had not put enough salt in the food, when she was late back from the well, or when she served him with cold food.

Lucy told her mother, who constantly told her to study her husband, learn his likes and dislikes and then try to be a good wife. After years of beating, in which he even damaged her eye, Lucy one day got an axe and while he slept, chopped off his head.

Lucy was charged with murder and in spite of the fact that she had two children, one a baby of two months, she was sentenced to 15 years' imprisonment. A friend has advised her to appeal against the sentence.

- What are Lucy's chances of succeeding on appeal?

- What reasons can Lucy raise in her defence against the conviction and sentence?

- Do you think the judge was fair to punish her in that way and what factors may have affected his decision?

- Would the judge's decision have been different if John had beaten Judy to death?

Critical Incident 1: Cohabitation

Ms Segale has lived with Mr Dimakatso for ten years. They have six children but they are not legally married. Last year Mr Dimakatso left home and is now living with another woman in another town. Ms. Segale is not working and three of the children are still young and attending school. She has no income to support the children. When she appealed to Mr Dimakatso's parents, they said:

'Did you ever see us at your parent's house, asking for a wife for my nephew? Forget it. You are not legally married. The best thing you can do is to hand over the children to their paternal grandmother.' Ms Segale is devastated.

- What are the issues and the root causes of the problem?

- How can Ms Segale be helped?

- Is it possible to influence the lawmakers in this case? If so, what are your suggestions?

- Which institution can take up the matter?

Critical Incident 2: Mild Slapping (Chastisement)

Mabel married Ben two years ago. One day he came back from work, changed his clothes and went away without saying where he was going. He returned at 4 a.m. and demanded a hot meal. She asked him where he had been and refused to wake up to warm up the food. He slapped her twice and told her that she was a useless wife. Mabel reported the problem to his mother. The next day, Ben's mother called him and asked him about the problem. Ben responded as follows:

'What are you going on about, mother? I did not attack Mabel. Do you see any bruises or signs of a fight on her body? I was just disciplining her. A wife must be disciplined if she neglects her husband.' Ben's mother did not reply.

- What in your opinion are the problems?

- Was Ben right in what he said? Support your answer.

- Has GBV occurred? Why?

- How can Mabel and Ben be helped?

- What is the law, or what should it be?

Critical Incident 3: Sexual Harassment

Maria has worked for Mr Jameson as his secretary for six months. Every time he calls her into his office, he calls her over to him and touches her breasts. Sometimes he holds her hands and fondles them. Maria was uncomfortable with her superior's behaviour and began to resist. Mr Jameson became angry and said:

'What is wrong with you? I am not doing anything that you are not used to. You had better decide whether you want to work for me or not.'

- What are the problems?

- Is Mr. Jameson right to behave in that way?

- How can such problems be solved?

- What should the law do here?

Key Informant Views

Rape

My sister was raped in 1995. At that time she was only seven years old. A man from outside the village came to my mother's house, while my mother was out at the bar. The man told my sister to come with him to the bakery and promised to buy her some bread and guava juice. She agreed and followed him.

After buying the stuff, he asked her to accompany him to see his girlfriend, but instead walked with her through a bushy area. When she pleaded to go home, he replied, "I'll take you later." He immediately tore off her clothes, threatened her with a knife and raped her. She reported the incident to her mother, who reported it to the police. The man was locked up in a cell for a few days and later released. Nothing came of the case. My sister is back at school doing Standard 7. (A community junior secondary school student in the village)

- What are the issues involved?

- What services are available for the victim and the perpetrator?

- What factors contributed to the release of perpetrator?

- Is the law adequate? If not, what needs to be done?

Marital Rape

My husband raped me several times, particularly when I was tired and did not want to have sex, because of his insults and harassment. One rape took place after he had beaten me. He pushed me down, ripped off my underwear, and raped me, despite my protests. (Testimony based on High Court records)

- What are the issues involved?

- What services are available for the victim and perpetrator?

- What are your views on marital rape?

- Is there a law that considers this act? If not, what can be done?

Incest

My 14-year-old daughter came to me in tears one morning and said, "Mom, please ask dad to beat me with a belt or a stick, next time he does not like what I have written in my books." I asked her what her father had been using to punish her. I discovered that he had been sexually abusing her for the last three months, almost every four days. (A mother)

Look, we do not like incest and it's time we got rid of it. This secrecy around incest is keeping it alive. The time has come to confront this abuse and condemn it openly. (Women's focus group in a large village)

Bringing out issues of incest does not reveal our secrets to outsiders. Women are the ones who guard this secret with their lives until death. Talking about these things will not undermine our community, because incest is happening all over our country. It has to be condemned, especially by women. We can no longer pretend that it does not exist.

The perpetrators of incest are fathers, grandfathers, uncles and cousins. They sexually abuse children from the age of 4 to 15 years. Villagers, teachers or the abused children themselves reported these cases. We give them medical attention and counselling, but there is a gap here. Often the police are not involved. (Social worker in a large village)

Incest is a disease and will not stop until the government takes serious steps against it. Incest is on the increase. It has nothing to do with culture. It is behavioural and needs to be stamped out. (Focus group of men in a large village)

- What is the difference between defilement and incest?
- Why do such acts occur?
- Does this happen in your communities?
- What do you think can be done to end these devastating acts of violence?
- Should the mother be regarded as a victim or perpetrator?
- Is there a law which relates to this? If not, how should the law treat it?

References

1. Agimba C., Butengwa F., Osakue G., Ndura S. *Legal Rights Awareness Among Women in Africa* (1994)

2. Bhuku Chuuu M. *International Human Rights, Law and Violence Against Women* (2000)

3. British Council. *Violence Against Women : A Briefing Document on International Issues* (1999)

4. Commonwealth Secretariat. *Advancing the Human Rights of Women* (Hong Kong May 1996)

5. Commonwealth Secretariat. *A Model for an Integrated Approach to Eliminating Violence Against Women* (2000)

6. Commonwealth Secretariat (Humphrey H. H.). *Assessing the Status of Women* (2nd edition 1996)

7. Commonwealth Secretariat (Butegwa F.). *Combating Violence Against Women. A Case for an Integrated Approach* (2000)

8. Commonwealth Secretariat. *Confronting Violence* (June 1992)

9. Commonwealth Secretariat. *Guidelines for Police Training and Violence Against Women and Child Abuse* (1999, 2nd Edition)

10. Commonwealth Secretariat. *Learning by Sharing* (1999)

11. Commonwealth Secretariat (Oguli Oumo M.). *National Workshop on an International Approach for Combating Gender Violence* (Lusaka 2000)

12. Commonwealth Secretariat (Oguli Oumo M.). *SADC Regional Training on an Integrated Approach for Combating Violence Against Women* (Maseru December 2000)

13. Commonwealth Secretariat. *Violence Against Women* (1994)

14. Coomaraswamy R. *Critical Issues Confronting Women in the Commonwealth, 2000.* Paper prepared for Commonwealth Ministries Responsible for Women's Affairs (April 2000)

15. Gender in Development Division. *The Forms and Extent of Violence Against Women in Zambia and the Girl Child* (February 1998)

16. Gumbaonzvanda N and Win E. J. *Strengthening Linkages for Women's Rights in Africa* (date?)

17. Gwaba M. M. *Gender in Development Division – 1997 SADC Declaration on Gender Development; 1998 Addendum on the Prevention and Eradication of Violence Against Women and Children/Analysis of the SADC Framework for Reporting in the Zambia Context* (1997, 1998)

18. International Commission of Jurists. *A Paralegal Trainer's Manual for Africa* (Geneva 1994)

19. International Women's Tribune Centre. *Rights of Women* (New York 1998)

20. Kameri Mbote P. *Violence Against Women in Kenya. An Analysis of Law, Policy and Institutions Legal Education Materials* (WILDAF Botswana 1996)

21. Match International Centre. *The End of Violence Against Women. African Women's Initiatives* (November 1994)

22. Okumu Wengi J. *Weeding the Millet Field. Women's Law and Grass Roots Justice in Uganda* (1997)

23. SADC Head of States of Government. *The Prevention and Eradication of Violence Against Women and Children* (September 1998)

24. Schuler M. *Freedom from Violence/Women's Strategies from Around the World* (1992)

25. Sibote. M. E. *Violence Against Women in Zambia, Nature, Causes, Extent and Consequences*

26. SIPU. *Handbook for Trainers* (1991)

27. Sokoni C.C.Z. *An Integrated Approach for Combating Violence Against Women in Zambia* (November 2000)

28. The International Centre for Criminal Law Reform and Criminal Justice Policy. *Model Strategies and Practical Measures on the Elimination of Violence Against Women in the Field of Crime, Prevention and Criminal Justice* (March 1998)

29. The Ministry of Gender, Labour and Social Development. *Gender-sensitive Legal Literacy for Sub-county Councillors* (April 2000)

30. The Ministry of Labour and Home Affairs, Women Affairs Department. *A Study on the Socio-economic Implications of Violence Against Women* (Botswana March 1999)

31. The United Nations Department of Public Information. *World Conference on Human Rights* (June 1993)

32. The United Nations Department of Public Information. *Platform for Action and the Beijing Declaration* (New York 1996)

33. Tomasenski K. *Women and Human Rights* (1993)

34. Tylon J. and Stewart S. *Sexual and Domestic Violence, Help, Recovery and Action in Zimbabwe* (1991)

35. United Nations. *United Nations Reference Guide in the Field of Human Rights* (New York 1993)

36. WILDAF. *Strengthening Linkages for Women's Rights in Africa*

37. Women in Law and Development in Africa (WILDAF). *The Private is Public* (1995)

38. Women, Law and Development International. *Women's Human Rights Step by Step* (1997)

39. World Campaign for Human Rights (United Nations). *Human Rights Communications Procedures* (1992)

40. World Campaign for Human Rights (United Nations). *Human Rights. The Africa Charter on Human and People's Rights* (New York 1990)

41. Zimba M.L.N. *Brief on the Strengthening of Laws, Enforcement Mechanisms and Support Systems Relating to Gender-based Violence and Violence Against Children* (November 2000)

4174